A Word About Weight Watchers

Since 1963, Weight Watchers has grown from a handful of people to millions of members annually. Although weight-loss and weight-management results vary by individual, we recommend that you attend Weight Watchers meetings, follow the Weight Watchers food plan, and participate in regular physical activity. For the Watchers meetings nearest you, call 1-800-651-6000. Visit our Web site at WeightWatchers.com and look for *Weight Watchers* Magazine in meetings and on the newsstand.

Weight Watchers Publishing Group
Creative and Editorial Director: Nancy Gagliardi
Production Manager: Alan Biederman
Office Manager/Publishing Assistant: Jenny Laboy-Brace
Editors: Carol Prager, Eileen Runyan
Art Director: Ed Melnitsky
Recipe Developers: David Bloom, Jean Kressy,
Maureen Luchejko, Eileen Runyan
Photography: Ann Stratton
Food Stylist: Michael Pedersen
Prop Stylist: Cathy Cook

FIRESIDE
Rockefeller Center
1230 Avenue of the Americas
New York, NY 10020

First Fireside Edition 2003
FIRESIDE and colophon are registered trademarks of Simon & Schuster, Inc.
WEIGHT WATCHERS is a registered trademark of
Weight Watchers International, Inc.
For information regarding special discounts for bulk purchases, please contact Simon & Schuster Special Sales at 1-800-456-6798 or business@simonandschuster.com.
Editorial and art produced by W/W Twentyfirst Corp., 747 Third Ave.,
New York, NY 10017.
Library of Congress Cataloging-in-Publication Data
Weight Watchers take-out tonight!: 150+ restaurant favorites to make at
  home, all 8 points or less/Weight Watchers International.—1st Fireside ed.
      p, cm.
  "A Fireside book."
Includes index.
  1. Reducing diets—Recipes. 2. Convenience foods. I. Title: Weight Watchers
takeout tonight. II. Weight Watchers International.
  RM222.2.W3283   2003   641.5'635—dc21   2002042948
Manufactured in the United States of America
10 9 8 7 6
ISBN 0-7432-4594-6

Recipe Symbols: 🍳 one pot 🔥 hot/fiery 🕑 20 minutes or less

WeightWatchers®

take-out tonight!
150+ restaurant favorites to make at home

A FIRESIDE BOOK • Published by Simon & Schuster • New York   London   Toronto   Sydney

introduction

It's been said over and over: We're overworked, overstressed, and overbooked. But the fact is that somewhere between office work and homework, cleaning and carpooling, running errands and running a house, you have to eat. Add a family into this chaotic equation and what's a stressed-out wife and mother to do?

Call for take-out.

Recent statistics confirm that ordering out is our generation's way of resolving the daily "What's for dinner?" dilemma. You've also probably noticed that it's possible to walk out of your local market with a fully cooked fresh dinner. Rotisserie chicken or sushi, anyone?

Yet the obvious question arises: How does all this taking out to eat in fit into your life if you're trying to lose weight? Most likely, not very well. It's no secret that whether it's take-out from your local Chinese hangout, the fancy gourmet market, or your town's new Mexican restaurant, portions, fat content, and calorie count of these speedy dishes are, in a word, big.

Welcome to **Take-Out Tonight! 150+ Restaurant Favorites to Make at Home.** We've re-created and reinterpreted you and your family's tasty take-out favorites, keeping fat, calories, and **POINTS** in mind so that when the craving hits for peanutty sesame noodles, creamy cannolis, filling fajitas, or tasty nachos, you can indulge in your favorites—guiltlessly.

Our luscious recipes focus on big flavors and feature ingredients that may be new to your cooking repertoire. That's why we've included plenty of helpful hints, as well as listings of the items you'll need to make your kitchen the perfect pantry for creating these delicious dishes at home.

So put down the menu of your favorite restaurant and scan our index for your favorite dish. With **Take-Out Tonight!** there's really no reason to order out—so get cooking.

Nancy Gagliardi
Editorial Director

contents

DISCARD

1 deli specials

Crumb-Topped Jumbo Bran Muffins

MAKES 6 SERVINGS

Oversize muffins sound like they should be off-limits, but not this recipe. Unprocessed bran, sold in boxes in your market's cereal aisle or in bulk at natural-food stores, provides lots of fiber in these oversize delights. Jumbo muffin tins are available at kitchen specialty shops. For smaller muffins, spoon the batter into a standard 12-cup muffin tin, bake about 23 minutes, and cut the **POINTS** in half.

2 tablespoons + ¼ cup all-purpose flour
2 tablespoons packed light brown sugar
1 tablespoon butter, cut in small pieces
2 tablespoons chopped walnuts
1½ cups unprocessed bran
1 cup whole-wheat flour
1 teaspoon baking soda
½ teaspoon baking powder
¼ teaspoon salt
1 large egg
2 egg whites
⅓ cup sugar
2 tablespoons molasses
1 cup fat-free buttermilk
⅔ cup golden raisins

1. Preheat the oven to 375° F. Spray a 6-jumbo-cup (1 cup each) nonstick muffin tin with nonstick spray (or line a 6-cup nonstick muffin tin with foil or paper liners).

2. To make the crumb topping, combine 2 tablespoons of the all-purpose flour and the brown sugar in a medium bowl. With a pastry blender, cut in the butter until the mixture is crumbly. Stir in the walnuts.

3. Combine the bran, whole-wheat flour, the remaining ¼ cup all-purpose flour, the baking soda, baking powder, and salt in a large bowl. With an electric mixer on medium speed, beat the egg, egg whites, sugar, and molasses in a large bowl until blended. Gradually beat in the buttermilk. Gradually add the bran mixture, mixing on low speed until just blended. Stir in the raisins.

4. Spoon the batter into the cups, filling each about half full. Sprinkle with the crumb topping. Bake until a toothpick inserted in a muffin comes out clean, about 25 minutes. Cool in the pan on a rack 5 minutes; remove from the pan and cool completely on the rack.

Per serving (1 jumbo muffin): 329 Cal, 6 g Fat, 2 g Sat Fat, 42 mg Chol, 481 mg Sod, 64 g Carb, 8 g Fib, 10 g Prot, 111 mg Calc. **POINTS: 6.**

clever cook's tip

Before pouring the molasses into the measuring spoon, spray the spoon with nonstick spray and the molasses will slide easily off.

**Crumb-Topped
Jumbo Bran Muffins**

Whole-Wheat Cranberry Scones

MAKES 10 SERVINGS

Scones, from the Scottish word *sconbrot* (meaning "fine white bread"), are traditionally cooked on a griddle. But varieties made nowadays are usually baked. The dough can be cut into individual shapes or patted into a circle and baked as one round. Before baking, cut the round into wedges, but do not separate them. While they are still warm, cut with a serrated knife.

1⅓ cups all-purpose flour
⅔ cup whole-wheat flour
¼ cup granulated sugar
2½ teaspoons baking powder
¼ teaspoon baking soda
¼ teaspoon salt
3 tablespoons butter, cut into small pieces
¼ cup sweetened dried cranberries
2 teaspoons grated orange rind
1 large egg, lightly beaten
½ cup fat-free buttermilk
1 teaspoon confectioners' sugar

1. Preheat the oven to 375° F. Line a baking sheet with parchment or wax paper.

2. Combine the all-purpose flour, whole-wheat flour, granulated sugar, baking powder, baking soda, and salt in a large bowl. With a pastry blender, cut in the butter until the mixture is crumbly.

3. Add the cranberries and orange rind and stir with a fork. Add the egg and buttermilk and stir with a fork until the dry ingredients are just moistened. Gather the mixture into a ball, place on the baking sheet, and pat into a 7-inch circle. Cut into 10 wedges with a knife dipped in flour. Do not separate the wedges. Bake until golden brown and a toothpick inserted in the center comes out clean, about 20 minutes. Transfer to a rack. Sift the confectioners' sugar over the top. Cut with a serrated knife and serve warm.

Per serving (1 wedge): 165 Cal, 4 g Fat, 2 g Sat Fat, 31 mg Chol, 205 mg Sod, 27 g Carb, 2 g Fib, 4 g Prot, 41 mg Calc. ***POINTS: 3.***

clever cook's tip

When grating oranges use only the colored part of the rind, which contains the flavorful oils, and not the underlying white pith, which is bitter.

Chicken Soup with Mushrooms and Barley

MAKES 4 SERVINGS

Comforting by the bowl and a cure for all that ails you, chicken soup is a favorite deli lunch. Our version with mushrooms and barley only makes it more appealing and brings the comfort home. If you're pressed for time and don't have leftover cooked chicken on hand, substitute 1 (10-ounce) can 98% fat-free chunk chicken breast in water, drained and flaked, for the cooked chicken breast.

2 teaspoons butter
½ pound white mushrooms, coarsely chopped
2 carrots, diced
4 cups low-sodium chicken broth
2 cups water
½ cup quick-cooking barley
¼ teaspoon salt
⅛ teaspoon freshly ground pepper
1½ cups chopped cooked chicken breast
⅓ cup chopped fresh flat-leaf parsley
3 tablespoons grated Parmesan cheese

1. Melt the butter in a nonstick Dutch oven over medium-low heat, then stir in the mushrooms and carrots. Cover and cook, stirring occasionally, until the mushrooms are softened, about 5 minutes.

2. Add the broth, water, barley, salt, and pepper; bring to a boil. Reduce the heat and simmer, covered, until the barley is tender, about 15 minutes.

3. Stir in the chicken, parsley, and Parmesan and simmer just until heated through, about 2 minutes.

Per serving (2 cups): 270 Cal, 7 g Fat, 3 g Sat Fat, 53 mg Chol, 401 mg Sod, 28 g Carb, 6 g Fib, 25 g Prot, 115 mg Calc. *POINTS: 5.*

clever cook's tip

Soups with grains such as barley or rice tend to thicken as they stand, so add 1 to 2 tablespoons water for each cup of soup before reheating this delicious leftover.

Corn, Potato, and Leek Chowder

MAKES 4 SERVINGS ☕

Starchy, low-moisture baking potatoes work well in this chowder. Unlike waxy potatoes, which hold their shape when cooked, baking potatoes tend to fall apart, which is ideal for thickening soups. Mashing the potatoes with a potato masher also helps the thickening process.

1 tablespoon butter

2 leeks (about ¾ pound), cleaned and sliced (white and light green parts only)

2 carrots, diced

1 celery stalk, diced

2 (½-pound) baking potatoes, peeled and diced

4 cups low-sodium chicken broth

1 cup water

½ teaspoon dried thyme

½ teaspoon salt

⅛ teaspoon freshly ground pepper

1 (10-ounce) package frozen corn kernels, thawed

1. Melt the butter in a nonstick Dutch oven over medium-high heat, then add the leeks, carrots, and celery. Cook, stirring frequently, until the leeks are softened, about 5 minutes. Add the potatoes, broth, water, thyme, salt, and pepper; bring to a boil. Reduce the heat and simmer, covered, until the potatoes are soft, about 20 minutes.

2. Add the corn and simmer, covered, about 2 minutes. Mash lightly with a potato masher to break up the potatoes.

Per serving (1½ cups): 245 Cal, 5 g Fat, 3 g Sat Fat, 12 mg Chol, 448 mg Sod, 46 g Carb, 6 g Fib, 8 g Prot, 69 mg Calc. *POINTS: 5.*

clever cook's tip

Because they grow in sandy soil, leeks need to be rinsed thoroughly. Trim off the root ends and dark green tops, leaving the white and light green parts. Slice thinly, place in a colander, and rinse under running water until there is no more sand. Drain well.

Corn, Potato, and Leek Chowder

Beef and Black Bean Chili

MAKES 4 SERVINGS

For a cool sidekick to this hot chili, top each serving with one-quarter of a peeled, diced avocado tossed with a little finely chopped red onion and fresh lime juice. Add 2 **POINTS** per serving.

½ **pound lean ground beef (10% or less fat)**
2 **onions, chopped**
2 **celery stalks, sliced**
1 **yellow bell pepper, seeded and diced**
1 **(10-ounce) package white mushrooms, quartered**
1 **jalapeño pepper, seeded and minced (wear gloves to prevent irritation)**
1 **large garlic clove, minced**
2 **(14½-ounce) cans diced tomatoes**
1 **(15½-ounce) can black beans, rinsed and drained**
3 **cups water**
2 **tablespoons tomato paste**
1½ **tablespoons chili powder**
1 **teaspoon ground cumin**
1 **teaspoon dried oregano, crumbled**
½ **teaspoon salt**
⅛ **teaspoon pepper**
3 **tablespoons chopped cilantro**

1. Spray a large nonstick saucepan with nonstick spray and set over medium-high heat. Add the beef and cook, breaking it up with a wooden spoon, until browned, 3–5 minutes. Drain off any fat.

2. Add the onions, celery, bell pepper, mushrooms, jalapeño, and garlic. Cook, stirring occasionally, until the vegetables are softened, about 8 minutes. Add the tomatoes, beans, water, tomato paste, chili powder, cumin, oregano, salt, and pepper; bring to a boil. Reduce the heat and simmer, uncovered, stirring occasionally, until the chili is thickened, about 45 minutes. Sprinkle with the cilantro and serve.

Per serving (2 cups): 244 Cal, 5 g Fat, 2 g Sat Fat, 15 mg Chol, 833 mg Sod, 38 g Carb, 12 g Fib, 18 g Prot, 115 mg Calc. **POINTS: 4.**

clever cook's tip

Crumbling the oregano leaves between your fingers as you add them to the pot helps release their flavor.

Roasted Red Pepper and Goat Cheese Sandwiches

Peppery arugula leaves add bite to this tangy goat cheese and roasted pepper combo. For a different flavor, substitute goat cheese flavored with herbs (such as dill) or cracked black pepper.

1 large red bell pepper, seeded and halved
¼ pound goat cheese, softened
4 whole-wheat English muffins, split and toasted
Arugula leaves

1. Preheat the broiler. Line a baking sheet with foil; place the bell pepper pieces, cut-side down, on a baking sheet. Broil 5 inches from the heat, turning occasionally with tongs, until lightly charred, about 10 minutes. Wrap the pieces in the foil and let steam for 20 minutes. When the pieces are cool enough to handle, peel and cut each piece in half.

2. Spread about 2 tablespoons goat cheese on the bottom half of each muffin. Top cheese with one piece of roasted pepper and several arugula leaves; cover sandwiches with muffin tops.

Per serving (1 sandwich): 249 Cal, 10 g Fat, 6 g Sat Fat, 22 mg Chol, 568 mg Sod, 30 g Carb, 5 g Fib, 12 g Prot, 269 mg Calc. *POINTS: 5.*

clever cook's tip

The bell pepper can be roasted ahead of time and refrigerated in a covered bowl. Before using, drain and blot with paper towels. If you like, roast 2 or 3 bell peppers at the same time and store them in the refrigerator for up to 1 week; use them in pasta sauces or other sandwiches throughout the week.

deli specials

Smoked Turkey Sandwiches with Chutney Mayonnaise

MAKES 4 SERVINGS 🕐

Although chutneys are traditionally served with curries, their sweet and tangy taste is well suited to other foods, including meat. A small amount of store-bought mango chutney stirred with mayonnaise is a quick and easy way to add flavor to this simple deli sandwich. Thinly sliced chicken breast can be substituted for the turkey.

¼ cup fat-free mayonnaise

2 tablespoons mango chutney

8 slices pumpernickel bread

6 ounces thinly sliced smoked turkey breast

1¼ cups thinly sliced English cucumber

2 cups alfalfa sprouts

12 grape tomatoes

1. Combine the mayonnaise and chutney in a small bowl.

2. Divide and spread the chutney mayonnaise on 4 slices of bread. Layer the turkey, cucumber, and sprouts over the top. Cover each sandwich with a slice of the remaining bread. Serve with the tomatoes.

Per serving (1 sandwich with 3 grape tomatoes): 217 Cal, 3 g Fat, 1 g Sat Fat, 18 mg Chol, 874 mg Sod, 37 g Carb, 5 g Fib, 14 g Prot, 53 mg Calc.
POINTS: 4.

Roast Beef Sandwiches with Caramelized Onions

MAKES 3 SERVINGS

When onions are cooked to the point where their natural sugars caramelize, or melt, they turn golden brown and their pungent taste is transformed into a mild sweetness. Caramelizing should not be hurried. It takes time, but the flavor payback is worth it. If you can't find the naturally sweet Vidalia onion, substitute 2 yellow onions and add 1 teaspoon of sugar.

1 teaspoon olive oil
1 Vidalia onion, cut vertically into thin strips
6 teaspoons honey mustard
6 slices rye bread
6 ounces thinly sliced lean roast beef

1. Heat a large nonstick skillet over medium-high heat. Swirl in the oil, then add the onion. Cook, stirring occasionally, until softened, about 8 minutes. Reduce the heat to low and cook, stirring occasionally, until the onion is golden brown, about 20 minutes.

2. Divide and spread the mustard on 3 slices of bread. Layer the beef and onions over the top. Cover each sandwich with a slice of the remaining bread.

Per serving (1 sandwich): 292 Cal, 7 g Fat, 2 g Sat Fat, 27 mg Chol, 1,022 mg Sod, 40 g Carb, 4 g Fib, 17 g Prot, 60 mg Calc. *POINTS: 6.*

clever cook's tip

For homemade honey mustard in a jiffy, stir together equal parts honey and mustard; store, refrigerated, in a tightly covered jar.

Tuna Melts with Asparagus

MAKES 4 SERVINGS

Adding asparagus to this American favorite is an easy way to get a nutrient boost. If you prefer, thinly sliced tomatoes or roasted bell peppers can be substituted for the asparagus.

1 (6-ounce) can water-packed tuna, drained and flaked

2 tablespoons minced celery

2 tablespoons fat-free mayonnaise

1 tablespoon fresh lemon juice

¼ teaspoon freshly ground pepper

32 thin asparagus spears (about 10 ounces), trimmed

4 slices whole-grain bread, toasted

4 (¾-ounce) slices part-skim mozzarella cheese

1. Combine the tuna, celery, mayonnaise, lemon juice, and pepper in a medium bowl.

2. Place the asparagus in a steamer basket; set in a saucepan over 1 inch of boiling water. Cover tightly and steam the asparagus until bright green and tender, about 1½ minutes. Blot dry with paper towels.

3. Preheat the broiler. Spread the tuna salad on the slices of toast. Layer with the asparagus and mozzarella. Arrange on a baking sheet and broil 3–4 inches from the heat until the cheese melts, about 1½ minutes.

Per serving (1 sandwich): 180 Cal, 5 g Fat, 3 g Sat Fat, 26 mg Chol, 386 mg Sod, 18 g Carb, 6 g Fib, 17 g Prot, 270 mg Calc. **POINTS: 3.**

clever cook's tip

Asparagus can range from pencil-thin to thick, but size has nothing to do with taste. When buying asparagus look for firm, straight spears with tightly closed tips, a sign of freshness. For even cooking, choose same-size spears.

Reuben Sandwiches

MAKES 4 SERVINGS 🕐

Stories abound about the origin of the Reuben sandwich. However, the most accurate tale about the popular corned beef, Swiss cheese, and sauerkraut on rye classic involves Sam Reuben, a New York City delicatessen owner. The sandwich was created in 1941 to honor Annette Seelos, an actress who ate at Reuben's restaurant. Rather than calling it the "Annette sandwich," Reuben named it after himself. Reuben sandwiches can be made with two slices of bread and grilled, or served open-face and baked until the cheese melts. In an authentic Reuben, the bread is spread with Russian dressing.

¼ cup fat-free mayonnaise

2 tablespoons chili sauce

4 slices rye bread

¼ pound thinly sliced lean corned beef

1 cup well-drained canned sauerkraut

2 ounces deli-thin Swiss cheese slices

1. Preheat the oven to 400° F.

2. Combine the mayonnaise and chili sauce in a small bowl. Spread the mayonnaise mixture on the bread. Layer with the corned beef, sauerkraut, and Swiss.

3. Place the sandwiches on a baking sheet. Bake until the cheese melts, about 3 minutes.

Per serving (1 open sandwich): 221 Cal, 10 g Fat, 4 g Sat Fat, 41 mg Chol, 1,105 mg Sod, 22 g Carb, 2 g Fib, 12 g Prot, 159 mg Calc. **POINTS: 5.**

the perfect pantry

Here are a few items you'll need to create great deli fare.

•**Chili sauce:** A spicy blend of tomatoes, chili powder, onions, green bell peppers, vinegar, sugar, and spices.

•**Honey mustard:** A blend of prepared mustard (often Dijon) and honey.

•**Lean corned beef:** Beef brisket or beef round cured in seasoned brine.

•**Pumpernickel bread:** Dark bread with a slightly sour taste; contains a large amount of rye flour and a small amount of wheat flour; molasses is added for color and flavor.

•**Rye bread:** A combination of rye flour, bread flour, and brown sugar; available with or without caraway seeds.

•**Sauerkraut:** A mixture of shredded cabbage, salt, and spices that's allowed to ferment; available fresh or in cans.

Hummus Club Sandwiches

MAKES 4 SERVINGS

Hummus, a popular Middle Eastern spread, is often served with pita wedges. Here, it makes a tasty base for a triple-decker vegetarian sandwich of lettuce, tomato, cucumber, and alfalfa sprouts.

½ (15½-ounce) can cannellini (white kidney) beans, rinsed and drained
1 small garlic clove, minced
1 tablespoon minced red onion
1½ teaspoons tahini
1½ teaspoons water
1 teaspoon fresh lemon juice
⅛ teaspoon salt
Pinch freshly ground pepper
6 slices whole-grain bread
1 small tomato, thinly sliced
2 Boston lettuce leaves
½ cup thinly sliced cucumber
1 cup alfalfa sprouts
2 tablespoons fat-free mayonnaise

1. To prepare the hummus, combine the beans, garlic, onion, tahini, water, lemon juice, salt, and pepper in a food processor; process to the consistency of a spread.

2. Spread the hummus on 2 slices of bread. Layer with tomato and lettuce. Top each with another slice of bread. Layer with cucumber and sprouts. Spread mayonnaise on the remaining bread, and top each sandwich with the bread. Cut each sandwich diagonally into quarters.

Per serving (2 quarters): 151 Cal, 2 g Fat, 0 g Sat Fat, 0 mg Chol, 337 mg Sod, 31 g Carb, 10 g Fib, 6 g Prot, 175 mg Calc. *POINTS: 2.*

clever cook's tip

Use the whole can of cannellini beans to make twice the amount of hummus, and store the remaining half, covered, in the refrigerator for up to 4 days. Hummus is an excellent dip for raw vegetables or pita wedges.

Tabbouleh with White Beans and Artichoke Hearts

MAKES 4 SERVINGS ⊘

Tabbouleh is a classic Middle Eastern salad made with bulgur, or wheat kernels that have been steamed, dried, and crushed. In our version, a traditional tabbouleh (with lots of parsley and mint and only a smattering of vegetables) has been transformed into a substantial main-dish salad with the addition of artichoke hearts and white beans.

2 cups water
⅔ cup bulgur
1 cup canned small white beans, rinsed and drained
1 (14-ounce) can artichoke hearts, drained and coarsely chopped
1 cup diced zucchini
2 plum tomatoes, diced
½ cup finely chopped fresh parsley
2 tablespoons fresh lemon juice
1 tablespoon extra-virgin olive oil
¼ teaspoon salt
¼ teaspoon coarsely ground black pepper
Boston lettuce leaves

1. Bring the water to a boil in a medium saucepan. Stir in the bulgur. Remove from the heat; cover and let stand until the bulgur is softened, 15–20 minutes. Drain into a strainer, pressing out any excess water with the back of a large spoon.

2. Transfer the drained bulgur to a large bowl. Add the beans, artichokes, zucchini, tomatoes, parsley, lemon juice, oil, salt, and pepper; toss to combine. Serve the salad, at room temperature, over the lettuce.

Per serving (1½ cups): 205 Cal, 4 g Fat, 1 g Sat Fat, 0 mg Chol, 342 mg Sod, 40 g Carb, 13 g Fib, 9 g Prot, 91 mg Calc. *POINTS: 4.*

clever cook's tip

Bulgur is available in fine, medium, and coarse grains. For this recipe the medium grain, sold in bulk in natural-food stores, works best. After soaking, ⅔ cup medium bulgur yields about 2 cups.

deli specials

Crunchy Chicken Salad Wraps

Crunchy Chicken Salad Wraps

MAKES 4 SERVINGS ⏱

In recent years, tortillas have outsold bagels and English muffins—not a surprising fact, given their great versatility. In the hands of a skilled cook, a tortilla can be turned into anything, from a taco to an enchilada to a quesadilla. In this recipe, they serve as a neat holder for chicken salad. The crunchy vegetables contrast nicely with the soft tortillas, and the salad can be made ahead and refrigerated until you are ready to assemble the wrap. Firm, crisp pickling cucumbers with small seeds can be substituted for the English cucumber, if you like.

1½ **cups chopped cooked chicken breast**
¼ **cup diced English cucumber**
¼ **cup minced celery**
2 **scallions, chopped**
1 **tablespoon finely chopped fresh flat-leaf parsley**
¼ **cup fat-free mayonnaise**
2 **tablespoons fresh lemon juice**
⅛ **teaspoon freshly ground pepper**
4 **(8-inch) fat-free flour tortillas**
4 **red-leaf lettuce leaves**

1. Combine the chicken, cucumber, celery, scallions, parsley, mayonnaise, lemon juice, and pepper in a medium bowl.

2. Warm the tortillas according to package directions. Divide and layer the lettuce and chicken mixture on the tortillas. Roll up, fasten with toothpicks, and cut diagonally in half.

Per serving (2 halves): 207 Cal, 2 g Fat, 0 g Sat Fat, 40 mg Chol, 302 mg Sod, 29 g Carb, 1 g Fib, 19 g Prot, 100 mg Calc. *POINTS: 4.*

Pesto Shrimp and Orzo Salad

MAKES 4 SERVINGS

When prepared the traditional way, pesto (meaning "to pound") is made by mashing fresh basil leaves in a mortar with a pestle. Today, most time-strapped cooks opt for a little help from a food processor or blender. For this recipe, you can use 3 tablespoons of our Homemade Pesto [see Fresh Fettuccine with Homemade Pesto, page 157]. Or, to save even more time, use store-bought pesto, which can be found in the supermarket refrigerator case. Pesto contains oil and nuts, both high in fat, but because it has such an intense flavor, only a few tablespoons are needed.

1 cup orzo
4 cups bite-size broccoli florets
1/3 cup fat-free mayonnaise
3 tablespoons prepared pesto
1/4 teaspoon salt
1/8 teaspoon freshly ground pepper
1/2 pound cooked shrimp, cut into bite-size pieces

1. Cook the orzo according to package directions; drain, reserving 2 tablespoons of the cooking liquid in a cup. Rinse the orzo under cool water until lukewarm, then drain well.
2. Put the broccoli in a steamer basket; set in a saucepan over 1 inch of boiling water. Cover tightly and steam the broccoli until bright green and crisp-tender, about 2 minutes. Rinse under cool water until lukewarm, then drain well.
3. Stir the mayonnaise, pesto, the 2 tablespoons of the reserved cooking liquid, salt, and pepper in a large bowl. Add the orzo, broccoli, and shrimp; toss to coat.

Per serving (1 1/2 cups): 305 Cal, 7 g Fat, 2 g Sat Fat, 114 mg Chol, 522 mg Sod, 40 g Carb, 3 g Fib, 22 g Prot, 147 mg Calc. **POINTS: 6.**

clever cook's tip

When buying broccoli, look for tightly closed dark green or purplish buds and crisp, slender stems. Florets with deeper colors have more nutrients than paler ones. Refrigerate the broccoli (unwashed) in a plastic bag in the crisper, where it will keep for 3 to 5 days (depending on how fresh it was when you bought it).

Lemon-Buttermilk Loaf

MAKES 12 SERVINGS

Don't be fooled by the word *buttermilk*. Made by adding lactic acid bacteria to milk (called culturing), buttermilk has little, if any, fat and is an excellent source of calcium. Buttermilk keeps well in the refrigerator but can separate, so shake it well before using.

1⅓ cups all-purpose flour
⅓ cup whole-wheat flour
1 teaspoon baking powder
¼ teaspoon baking soda
⅛ teaspoon salt
5 tablespoons butter, softened
1 cup granulated sugar
1 large egg
2 egg whites
1 tablespoon grated lemon rind
1 teaspoon vanilla extract
¾ cup fat-free buttermilk
½ cup sifted confectioners' sugar
1 tablespoon fresh lemon juice

1. Preheat the oven to 350° F. Spray an 4 x 8-inch loaf pan with nonstick spray. Fold a 15-inch sheet of wax paper lengthwise to 7 inches wide; line the bottom and sides of the pan with the wax paper.

2. Combine the flour, whole-wheat flour, baking powder, baking soda, and salt in a large bowl.

3. With an electric mixer on medium speed, beat the butter, granulated sugar, egg, egg whites, lemon rind, and vanilla in another large bowl until well blended. With the mixer on low speed, add the flour mixture alternately with the buttermilk and mix until just combined. Pour the batter into the pan and bake until a toothpick inserted in the center comes out clean, about 55 minutes. Transfer the pan to a rack.

4. Combine the confectioners' sugar and lemon juice in a small bowl and stir until smooth. Spread over the top of the hot loaf and let cool 20 minutes. Remove the loaf from the pan, peel off the wax paper, and cool completely on the rack.

Per serving (¹⁄₁₂ of loaf): 203 Cal, 6 g Fat, 3 g Sat Fat, 31 mg Chol, 114 mg Sod, 35 g Carb, 1 g Fib, 4 g Prot, 31 mg Calc. ***POINTS: 4.***

clever cook's tip

Lining the pan with wax paper makes it easy to remove the cake from the pan. Run a thin spatula between the paper and the pan at the ends, then lift out the cake and peel away the paper.

2 chinese classics

Wonton Soup

This classic soup shows the skillful use of contrasting flavors and textures that is typical of Chinese cooking. We've included bok choy for a nutrient boost. Bok choy is a mild-flavored vegetable with crunchy stalks and tender dark green leaves. It is available year-round in most supermarkets or Asian groceries.

WONTONS

- ¼ **pound ground skinless chicken breast**
- 2 **scallions, finely chopped**
- 1 **teaspoon minced peeled fresh ginger**
- 1 **teaspoon reduced-sodium soy sauce**
- 1 **teaspoon cornstarch**
- ¼ **teaspoon Asian (dark) sesame oil**
- ⅛ **teaspoon salt**
- ⅛ **teaspoon freshly ground pepper**
- 16 **(3-inch) square wonton wrappers**

SOUP

- 4 **cups low-sodium chicken broth**
- 1 **tablespoon reduced-sodium soy sauce**
- ½ **pound bok choy, coarsely chopped (about 2 cups)**
- 4 **scallions, cut into ½-inch pieces**

1. To prepare the wontons, combine the chicken, scallions, ginger, soy sauce, cornstarch, sesame oil, salt, and pepper in a bowl; set aside.

2. Arrange 8 wonton wrappers on a work surface. Place 1 teaspoon of the chicken mixture in the center of each wrapper. Moisten the edges of each wonton wrapper with water and pull one of the top corners diagonally over the filling to make a triangle. Press the edges firmly to seal. Bring left and right corners together above the filling. Overlap the tips of these corners, moisten with water, and press together. Place completed wontons on a baking sheet lightly covered with cornstarch and cover with damp paper towels. Repeat with the remaining filling and wrappers, making 16 wontons.

3. To prepare the soup, bring the broth and soy sauce to a boil in a large saucepan. Reduce the heat to medium-low and add the wontons and bok choy; simmer, stirring occasionally, until the wontons are cooked through and the bok choy is tender, about 10 minutes. Sprinkle with the scallions and serve.

Per serving (1 cup soup with 4 wontons): 179 Cal, 3 g Fat, 1 g Sat Fat, 22 mg Chol, 769 mg Sod, 24 g Carb, 2 g Fib, 14 g Prot, 106 mg Calc. *POINTS: 3.*

Hot-and-Sour Soup

MAKES 4 SERVINGS

Traditionally served as a Chinese banquet dish, hot-and-sour soup is the perfect chill-chaser to make on a cold winter evening. The chili-garlic sauce—found in bottles or jars in the Asian section of most supermarkets—adds just the right kick, and the wood-ear mushrooms lend an air of the exotic. Wood-ear mushrooms, also known as black or tree fungus, can usually be found in the dried-mushroom section of your supermarket's produce department.

6 dried wood-ear mushrooms

4 cups low-sodium chicken broth

2 tablespoons reduced-sodium soy sauce

1 tablespoon chili-garlic sauce

3 tablespoons rice vinegar

1 teaspoon Asian (dark) sesame oil

½ pound reduced-fat soft tofu, drained and cut into ½-inch cubes

1 (8-ounce) can bamboo shoots, drained and thinly sliced

2½ tablespoons cornstarch

3 tablespoons water

1 egg white, lightly beaten with 1 tablespoon water

1. Combine the wood-ear mushrooms with enough hot water to cover by 2 inches in a small bowl; let stand 15 minutes, then drain.

2. Bring the broth, soy sauce, chili-garlic sauce, vinegar, and sesame oil to a boil in a large saucepan. Add the drained mushrooms, tofu, and bamboo shoots. Reduce the heat and simmer 10 minutes. Combine the cornstarch and water in a small bowl; stir in about ¼ cup of the hot liquid, then return to the pan. Cook, stirring constantly, until the mixture boils and thickens slightly, about 1 minute. Remove from the heat; slowly drizzle the egg mixture into the soup while stirring in a circular motion. Serve at once.

Per serving (1⅓ cups): 124 Cal, 4 g Fat, 1 g Sat Fat, 4 mg Chol, 794 mg Sod, 14 g Carb, 5 g Fib, 10 g Prot, 30 mg Calc. **POINTS: 2.**

clever cook's tip

To freeze, simply cool the soup to room temperature and transfer to plastic containers. Be sure to leave ½-inch clearance at the top of each container to allow for expansion as the soup freezes. If you can't find wood-ear mushrooms in your market, purchase them on-line from www.asiafoods.com.

chinese classics

Hot-and-Sour Soup
and Pan-Steamed
Vegetable Dumplings
with Soy Dipping Sauce

Pan-Steamed Vegetable Dumplings with Soy Dipping Sauce

MAKES 45 DUMPLINGS

These dumplings are cocktail-party perfect. Serve them on a bamboo tray, and place the dipping sauce in an Asian teacup or a ramekin. You can find wonton wrappers in the refrigerator case of most supermarkets and Asian groceries.

DIPPING SAUCE

- 6 tablespoons lite soy sauce
- 1½ tablespoons rice vinegar
- 2¼ teaspoons minced peeled fresh ginger
- 1 garlic clove, minced
- 1½ teaspoons sugar
- 1½ teaspoons Asian (dark) sesame oil
- ⅛ teaspoon pepper

DUMPLINGS

- 2 teaspoons canola oil
- 1 teaspoon Asian (dark) sesame oil
- 2 tablespoons minced peeled fresh ginger
- 3 garlic cloves, minced
- ½ pound shiitake mushrooms, thinly sliced
- 3 cups shredded Chinese cabbage
- 2 tablespoons sake
- 3 scallions, chopped
- 1 carrot, shredded
- 1 tablespoon lite soy sauce
- 45 (3-inch) round wonton wrappers

1. To prepare the dipping sauce, combine the soy sauce, vinegar, ginger, garlic, sugar, sesame oil, and pepper in a small bowl; set aside.

2. To prepare the dumplings, heat a nonstick wok or a large, deep skillet over medium-high heat until a drop of water sizzles. Swirl in the canola and sesame oil, then add the ginger and garlic. Stir-fry until fragrant, about 10 seconds. Stir in the mushrooms and cabbage, stir-fry until softened, about 3 minutes. Add the sake and cook, stirring often, until the liquid evaporates, 3–4 minutes. Add the scallions and carrot; stir-fry until softened, about 2 minutes. Remove from the heat and stir in the soy sauce. Transfer to a large bowl and let cool 10 minutes.

3. Arrange 6 wonton wrappers on a work surface. Place 1 teaspoon of the vegetable mixture in the center of each wrapper. Brush the edges of each wonton wrapper with water, then fold into half circles, pressing the edges to seal. Place the completed dumplings on a baking sheet lightly covered with cornstarch and cover with damp paper towels. Repeat with the remaining filling and wrappers, making a total of 45 dumplings.

4. Spray a large nonstick skillet with nonstick spray and set over medium-high heat. Add 10–12 dumplings to the skillet (don't overcrowd the pan or the dumplings won't brown) and cook until lightly browned on one side, 1 minute. Add ⅓ cup water to the skillet and cover it with a tight-fitting lid. Reduce the heat to medium, and cook the dumplings until the liquid evaporates, 3–4 minutes. Transfer the dumplings, browned-side up, to a serving tray. Serve with the dipping sauce.

Per serving (3 dumplings with ½ tablespoon dipping sauce): 101 Cal, 2 g Fat, 0 g Sat Fat, 2 mg Chol, 433 mg Sod, 18 g Carb, 1 g Fib, 3 g Prot, 31 mg Calc. ***POINTS: 2.***

Cold Sesame Noodles

Traditionally made with toasted sesame paste, this side dish is also terrific prepared with reduced-fat peanut butter. For best results, serve at room temperature soon after tossing the sauce with the noodles. If you like, serve it as a main dish for four people and sprinkle with a few chopped peanuts or toasted sesame seeds.

6 ounces chow mein noodles or spaghetti
⅓ cup reduced-fat smooth peanut butter
⅓ cup water
3 tablespoons ketchup
2 tablespoons hoisin sauce
2 tablespoons reduced-sodium soy sauce
2 tablespoons packed light brown sugar
1 tablespoon rice vinegar
1 teaspoon Asian (dark) sesame oil
2 scallions, chopped

1. Cook the noodles or spaghetti according to package directions; drain, rinse with cold water, and set aside.

2. Combine the peanut butter, water, ketchup, hoisin sauce, soy sauce, sugar, vinegar, and sesame oil in a small saucepan. Bring to a boil over medium-high heat, stirring constantly, until well mixed. Remove from the heat and cool about 10 minutes. Toss the noodles with the sauce, sprinkle with the scallions, and serve.

Per serving (⅓ cup): 182 Cal, 5 g Fat, 1 g Sat Fat, 0 mg Chol, 349 mg Sod, 29 g Carb, 2 g Fib, 6 g Prot, 12 mg Calc. *POINTS: 4.*

Shrimp-and-Pork Wontons

MAKES 40 WONTONS

Wontons make a wonderful party hors d'oeuvre. Put them out in a bamboo steamer, but first remember to brush the bamboo slats with a little sesame oil to prevent the wontons from sticking.

½ **pound medium shrimp, peeled, deveined, and finely chopped**

¼ **pound pork tenderloin, trimmed of all visible fat and finely chopped**

4 **scallions, chopped**

2 **tablespoons cornstarch**

1 **garlic clove, minced**

1 **tablespoon hoisin sauce**

2 **teaspoons Asian (dark) sesame oil**

1 **teaspoon reduced-sodium soy sauce**

40 **(3-inch) square wonton wrappers**

1. Combine the shrimp, pork, scallions, cornstarch, garlic, hoisin sauce, 1 teaspoon of the sesame oil, and the soy sauce in a medium bowl; set aside.

2. Arrange 6 wonton wrappers on a work surface. Place 1½ teaspoons of the shrimp mixture in the center of each wrapper. Moisten the edges of each wonton wrapper with water and pull one of the top corners diagonally over the filling to make a triangle. Press the edges firmly to seal. Bring left and right corners together above the filling. Overlap the tips of these corners, moisten with water, and press together. Place completed wontons on a baking sheet lightly covered with cornstarch and cover with damp paper towels. Repeat with the remaining filling and wrappers, making a total of 40 wontons.

3. Bring a large pot of water to a boil. Add the wontons, 20 at a time, to the pot; return to a boil, stirring occasionally. Cook until the wontons float to the top, about 1 minute. Remove with a slotted spoon and drain; toss the wontons with the remaining 1 teaspoon sesame oil to keep them from sticking together.

Per serving (2 wontons): 70 Cal, 1 g Fat, 0 g Sat Fat, 18 mg Chol, 133 mg Sod, 11 g Carb, 0 g Fib, 4 g Prot, 13 mg Calc. ***POINTS: 1.***

clever cook's tip

To create a flavorful dipping sauce, mix some finely chopped scallions with a little reduced-sodium soy sauce.

Broccoli with Garlic Sauce

MAKES 4 SERVINGS ⏱

To make this dish a vegetarian entrée, substitute vegetable broth for the chicken broth and hoisin sauce for the oyster sauce. For a protein boost and an extra 2 **POINTS** per serving, add ¾ pound of cubed firm tofu along with the broccoli.

½ cup low-sodium chicken broth

3 tablespoons sake or rice wine

2 tablespoons reduced-sodium soy sauce

2 tablespoons oyster sauce

1 tablespoon cornstarch

2 teaspoons sugar

1 tablespoon canola oil

3 garlic cloves, minced

1 pound broccoli crowns, cut into florets (4 cups)

1. Combine the broth, sake or rice wine, soy sauce, oyster sauce, cornstarch, and sugar in a small bowl; set aside.

2. Heat a nonstick wok or a large, deep skillet over medium-high heat until a drop of water sizzles. Swirl in the oil, then add the garlic. Stir-fry until fragrant, about 10 seconds. Add the broccoli and stir-fry until crisp-tender, about 3 minutes. Add the broth mixture and cook, stirring constantly, until the mixture boils and thickens, about 1 minute.

Per serving (¾ cup): 79 Cal, 4 g Fat, 0 g Sat Fat, 1 mg Chol, 390 mg Sod, 9 g Carb, 2 g Fib, 3 g Prot, 41 mg Calc. **POINTS: 2.**

clever cook's tip

This versatile garlic sauce works equally well with fresh green beans, asparagus, or snow peas instead of the broccoli.

Buddha's Delight

MAKES 4 SERVINGS

The true version of Buddha's Delight, which contains many dried ingredients (such as dried oysters, bean curd, and gingko nuts) that must be presoaked, is traditionally served on Chinese New Year. Here is today's popular version using fresh vegetables.

½ cup low-sodium chicken broth

¼ cup hoisin sauce

1 tablespoon reduced-sodium soy sauce

2 teaspoons cornstarch

1 tablespoon Asian (dark) sesame oil

1 onion, chopped

1 pound asparagus, trimmed and cut on a diagonal into 1-inch pieces

1 (10-ounce) container white mushrooms, sliced

1 red bell pepper, seeded and cut into ½-inch pieces

1 (8-ounce) can sliced water chestnuts, drained

3 scallions, chopped

2 cups cooked brown rice

1. Combine the broth, hoisin sauce, soy sauce, and cornstarch in a small bowl; set aside.

2. Heat a nonstick wok or a large, deep skillet over medium-high heat until a drop of water sizzles. Swirl in the oil, then add the onion. Stir-fry 1 minute. Add the asparagus, mushrooms, bell pepper, and water chestnuts. Stir-fry until crisp-tender, about 4 minutes. Add the broth mixture and cook, stirring constantly, until the mixture boils and thickens, about 2 minutes. Remove from the heat and stir in the scallions. Serve over the rice.

Per serving (1 cup vegetables with ½ cup rice): 259 Cal, 6 g Fat, 1 g Sat Fat, 1 mg Chol, 445 mg Sod, 47 g Carb, 7 g Fib, 8 g Prot, 49 mg Calc. *POINTS: 5.*

clever cook's tip

Follow the lead of many Chinese restaurants by giving your family the option to add tofu to this vegetable delight. Adding ¾ pound of cubed firm tofu to the broth mixture will add 2 *POINTS* to each serving.

Ma Po Tofu

According to Chinese folklore, a mysterious Mrs. Chen is the originator of this tasty tofu dish. If shitake mushrooms are unavailable, substitute an equal amount of white.

⅔ cup long-grain white rice

2 teaspoons Asian (dark) sesame oil

3 scallions, chopped

3 garlic cloves, minced

1 tablespoon minced peeled fresh ginger

¼ pound shiitake mushrooms, stemmed and thinly sliced

1 pound low-fat firm tofu, cut into ½-inch cubes

¾ cup low-sodium chicken broth

3 tablespoons reduced-sodium soy sauce

2 tablespoons sake or rice wine

2 teaspoons cornstarch

1 tablespoon water

1. Cook the rice according to package directions.

2. Heat a nonstick wok or a large, deep skillet over medium-high heat until a drop of water sizzles. Swirl in the oil, then add the scallions, garlic, and ginger. Stir-fry until fragrant, about 10 seconds. Add the mushrooms and stir-fry 2 minutes. Add the tofu, broth, soy sauce, and sake or rice wine; bring to a boil. Reduce the heat and simmer 5 minutes.

3. Combine the cornstarch and water in a small bowl; stir in about ¼ cup of the hot broth mixture, then return to the wok. Cook, stirring constantly, until the mixture boils and thickens, about 1 minute. Serve with the rice.

Per serving (¾ cup tofu mixture with ½ cup rice): 224 Cal, 4 g Fat, 1 g Sat Fat, 1 mg Chol, 574 mg Sod, 35 g Carb, 1 g Fib, 12 g Prot, 65 mg Calc. *POINTS: 5.*

Hunan Shrimp

MAKES 4 SERVINGS

Many of the dishes of the Hunan province of China are fiery. This Hunan specialty is a zesty blend of shrimp and chili-garlic sauce mellowed with black bean sauce and fresh vegetables. If you prefer, use half sea scallops and half shrimp.

1 pound medium shrimp, peeled and deveined
1 tablespoon + 2 teaspoons cornstarch
½ cup low-sodium chicken broth
2 tablespoons reduced-sodium soy sauce
1 tablespoon black bean sauce
1 tablespoon chili-garlic sauce
1 tablespoon canola oil
2 tablespoons minced peeled fresh ginger
1 onion, cut into ¼-inch slices
1 red bell pepper, seeded and cut into thin strips
1 green bell pepper, seeded and cut into thin strips
½ pound asparagus, trimmed and cut into 1-inch pieces
2 cups cooked brown rice

1. Combine the shrimp with 1 tablespoon of the cornstarch in a medium bowl; toss well to coat and set aside. Combine the broth, soy sauce, black bean sauce, chili-garlic sauce, and the remaining 2 teaspoons cornstarch in a small bowl; set aside.

2. Heat a nonstick wok or a large, deep skillet over medium-high heat until a drop of water sizzles. Swirl in 2 teaspoons of the oil, then add the shrimp. Stir-fry until just opaque in the center, about 3 minutes; transfer to a plate. Swirl in the remaining 1 teaspoon oil, then add the ginger and onion. Stir-fry until fragrant, about 1 minute. Add the bell peppers and asparagus; stir-fry until crisp-tender, about 2 minutes. Add the shrimp and broth mixture. Cook, stirring constantly, until the mixture boils and thickens, about 1 minute. Serve over the rice.

Per serving (1¼ cups shrimp mixture with ½ cup rice): 270 Cal, 6 g Fat, 1 g Sat Fat, 135 mg Chol, 667 mg Sod, 35 g Carb, 4 g Fib, 20 g Prot, 57 mg Calc. *POINTS: 5.*

clever cook's tip

For a shortcut, pick up precut vegetables from the supermarket salad bar when you buy the shrimp. You can also substitute broccoli florets or fresh snow peas for the asparagus, if they are unavailable.

chinese classics

Kung Pao Shrimp

MAKES 4 SERVINGS 🔥

Kung Pao Shrimp is exquisitely flavorful but quite spicy. If you don't care for spicy food but would love to try this dish, cut the chili-garlic sauce to 1 teaspoon, or leave it out entirely and add an extra minced garlic clove.

- ¾ **cup low-sodium chicken broth**
- ¼ **cup sake or rice wine**
- 2 **tablespoons reduced-sodium soy sauce**
- 2 **tablespoons honey**
- 1 **tablespoon chili-garlic sauce**
- 1 **tablespoon cornstarch**
- 1 **teaspoon Asian (dark) sesame oil**
- 2 **teaspoons canola oil**
- 1 **pound medium shrimp, peeled and deveined**
- 3 **scallions, chopped**
- 2 **tablespoons minced peeled fresh ginger**
- 2 **garlic cloves, minced**
- 4 **cups broccoli florets**
- 1 **(8-ounce) can bamboo shoots, drained**

1. Combine the broth, sake or rice wine, soy sauce, honey, chili-garlic sauce, cornstarch, and sesame oil in a bowl; set aside.

2. Heat a nonstick wok or a large, deep skillet over medium-high heat until a drop of water sizzles. Swirl in the canola oil, then add the shrimp. Stir-fry until just opaque in the center, about 3 minutes; transfer to a plate. Add the scallions, ginger, and garlic; stir-fry until fragrant, about 30 seconds. Add the broccoli florets and bamboo shoots; stir-fry until crisp-tender, about 2 minutes. Add the broth mixture and the shrimp. Cook, stirring constantly, until the mixture boils and thickens, about 1 minute.

Per serving (1¼ cups): 188 Cal, 5 g Fat, 1 g Sat Fat, 135 mg Chol, 661 mg Sod, 19 g Carb, 3 g Fib, 19 g Prot, 78 mg Calc. ***POINTS: 4.***

Kung Pao Shrimp

Shrimp Fried Rice

MAKES 6 SERVINGS

You can assemble this tasty dish in minutes when you buy shrimp already peeled and deveined. For best results, use rice that you've cooked the day before, since day-old rice is drier and makes better fried rice.

4 teaspoons canola oil

1 pound large shrimp, peeled and deveined

2 large eggs, lightly beaten

6 scallions, chopped

1 tablespoon grated peeled fresh ginger

1 cup frozen peas and carrots, thawed

4 cups cooked white rice

2 tablespoons reduced-sodium soy sauce

1 tablespoon hoisin sauce

1 teaspoon Asian (dark) sesame oil

½ teaspoon salt

1. Heat a nonstick wok or a large, deep skillet over medium-high heat until a drop of water sizzles. Swirl in 1 teaspoon of the canola oil, then add the shrimp. Stir-fry until golden and just opaque in the center, 4–5 minutes; transfer to a bowl.

2. Swirl 1 teaspoon of the canola oil into the wok. Add the eggs and cook, stirring until scrambled, about 2 minutes. Transfer the eggs to the bowl with the shrimp.

3. Swirl the remaining 2 teaspoons canola oil into the wok. Add the scallions and ginger. Stir-fry until softened, 1–2 minutes. Add the peas and carrots, shrimp, and scrambled egg; stir-fry, about 1 minute. Add the rice and stir-fry until heated through, 2–3 minutes. Stir in the soy sauce, hoisin sauce, sesame oil, and salt. Stir-fry until well combined and the rice mixture is hot, about 2 minutes.

Per serving (1 cup): 267 Cal, 7 g Fat, 1 g Sat Fat, 161 mg Chol, 584 mg Sod, 35 g Carb, 2 g Fib, 16 g Prot, 53 mg Calc. **POINTS: 6.**

Shrimp with Snow Peas

MAKES 4 SERVINGS ⏱

This simple yet satisfying dish is ready in less than 15 minutes. Serve it with boil-in-a-bag instant brown rice, which cooks in about 10 minutes.

1 **pound medium shrimp, peeled and deveined**

1 **tablespoon + 2 teaspoons cornstarch**

½ **cup low-sodium chicken broth**

3 **tablespoons reduced-sodium soy sauce**

1 **teaspoon sugar**

½ **teaspoon Asian (dark) sesame oil**

1 **tablespoon canola oil**

1 **(8-ounce) can sliced water chestnuts, drained**

2 **scallions, chopped**

2 **tablespoons minced peeled fresh ginger**

½ **pound fresh snow peas, trimmed**

2 **cups cooked instant brown rice**

1. Combine the shrimp with 1 tablespoon of the cornstarch in a medium bowl; toss well to coat and set aside. Combine the broth, soy sauce, sugar, sesame oil, and the remaining 2 teaspoons cornstarch in a small bowl; set aside.

2. Heat a nonstick wok or a large, deep skillet over medium-high heat until a drop of water sizzles. Swirl in the canola oil, then add the shrimp. Stir-fry until just opaque in the center, about 3 minutes; transfer to a plate.

3. Add the water chestnuts, scallions, and ginger; stir-fry until fragrant, about 30 seconds. Add the snow peas and stir-fry until crisp-tender, about 1 minute. Add the shrimp and broth mixture. Cook, stirring constantly, until the mixture boils and thickens, about 1 minute. Serve over the rice.

Per serving (1¼ cups shrimp mixture with ½ cup rice): 291 Cal, 6 g Fat, 1 g Sat Fat, 135 mg Chol, 637 mg Sod, 37 g Carb, 5 g Fib, 20 g Prot, 56 mg Calc. **POINTS: 6.**

Chicken Chow Mein

MAKES 4 SERVINGS

A harmonious blend of chicken, noodles, and simple vegetables makes this a perennial favorite. In traditional Chinese cooking, *mein* denotes that the noodles are made from wheat flour. If you are unable to find chow mein noodles, thin spaghetti or fettuccine work just as well.

6 ounces chow mein noodles or thin spaghetti

²⁄₃ cup low-sodium chicken broth

2 tablespoons dry sherry

2 teaspoons cornstarch

½ teaspoon salt

3 teaspoons canola oil

1 pound skinless boneless chicken breasts, cut into thin strips

1 onion, chopped

1 tablespoons minced peeled fresh ginger

3 garlic cloves, minced

1 green bell pepper, seeded and chopped

1 celery stalk, chopped

1. Cook the chow mein noodles or spaghetti according to package directions; drain.

2. Combine the broth, sherry, cornstarch, and salt in a small bowl; set aside.

3. Heat a nonstick wok or a large, deep skillet over high heat until a drop of water sizzles. Swirl in 2 teaspoons of the oil, then add the chicken. Stir-fry until just cooked through, 4–5 minutes. Transfer to a plate.

4. Swirl the remaining 1 teaspoon oil into the wok, then add the onion, ginger, and garlic. Stir-fry until fragrant, about 1 minute. Add the bell pepper and celery; stir-fry until crisp-tender, about 2 minutes. Add the chicken and broth mixture. Cook, stirring constantly, until the mixture boils and thickens, about 2 minutes. Serve over the cooked noodles.

Per serving (1¼ cups): 359 Cal, 7 g Fat, 1 g Sat Fat, 63 mg Chol, 379 mg Sod, 42 g Carb, 4 g Fib, 30 g Prot, 42 mg Calc. ***POINTS: 7.***

clever cook's tip

Fresh ginger must be peeled before using. Peel a chunk of ginger, wrap it in plastic wrap, and keep it in the freezer for up to 3 months. Slice off a portion of the frozen ginger as needed.

Chicken with Black Bean Sauce

MAKES 4 SERVINGS

Black bean sauce, sesame oil, ginger, and garlic all work together deliciously to give rich flavor to this chicken dish. Black bean sauce, a favorite Chinese seasoning ingredient, is made from Chinese black beans, which are fermented and seasoned with salt and spices.

1 **pound skinless boneless chicken breasts, cut into thin strips**
2 **tablespoons cornstarch**
½ **cup low-sodium chicken broth**
2 **tablespoons black bean sauce**
1 **tablespoon reduced-sodium soy sauce**
1 **tablespoon sugar**
1 **tablespoon Asian (dark) sesame oil**
1 **tablespoon minced peeled fresh ginger**
3 **garlic cloves, minced**
¼ **pound white mushrooms, quartered**
¼ **pound fresh snow peas, trimmed and halved**
1 **carrot, thinly sliced**

1. Combine the chicken with 1 tablespoon of the cornstarch in a medium bowl; toss well to coat and set aside. Combine the remaining 1 tablespoon cornstarch, the broth, black bean sauce, soy sauce, and sugar in a small bowl; set aside.

2. Heat a nonstick wok or a large, deep skillet over medium-high heat until a drop of water sizzles. Swirl in the oil, then add the chicken. Stir-fry until lightly browned, 2–3 minutes. Add the ginger and garlic; stir-fry until fragrant, about 30 seconds. Add the mushrooms, snow peas, and carrot; stir-fry until crisp-tender, about 3 minutes. Add the broth mixture and cook, stirring constantly, until the mixture boils and thickens, and the chicken is just cooked through, 1–2 minutes.

Per serving (1 cup): 223 Cal, 7 g Fat, 1 g Sat Fat, 63 mg Chol, 286 mg Sod, 14 g Carb, 2 g Fib, 26 g Prot, 37 mg Calc. *POINTS: 5.*

clever cook's tip

Shop carefully when buying soy sauce: For superior flavor, it should be made from soy and not hydrolyzed vegetable protein.

chinese classics

General Tso's Chicken

MAKES 4 SERVINGS ♦

This wonderful dish originated in China's Hunan province and demonstrates the Chinese tradition of naming dishes after significant figures.

1 pound skinless boneless chicken breasts, cut into 1-inch chunks

5 tablespoons dry sherry

1 tablespoon + 2 teaspoons cornstarch

1 tablespoon oyster sauce

2 tablespoons water

2 tablespoons reduced-sodium soy sauce

1 tablespoon honey

1 tablespoon rice vinegar

1 teaspoon Asian (dark) sesame oil

2 teaspoons canola oil

1 tablespoon minced peeled fresh ginger

2 garlic cloves, minced

3 scallions, chopped

½ teaspoon crushed red pepper

2 celery stalks, chopped

1 red bell pepper, seeded and chopped

1. Combine the chicken, 2 tablespoons of the sherry, 1 tablespoon of the cornstarch, and the oyster sauce in a medium bowl; set aside to marinate for 5 minutes.

2. Combine the remaining 3 tablespoons sherry, the water, soy sauce, honey, rice vinegar, sesame oil, and the remaining 2 teaspoons cornstarch in a small bowl; set aside.

3. Heat a nonstick wok or a large, deep skillet over medium-high heat until a drop of water sizzles. Swirl in the canola oil, then add the chicken mixture. Stir-fry until lightly browned, 2–3 minutes. Add the ginger, garlic, scallions, and crushed red pepper; stir-fry until fragrant, about 30 seconds. Add the celery and bell pepper; stir-fry until crisp-tender, 2–3 minutes. Stir in the sherry mixture and cook, stirring constantly, until the mixture boils and thickens, and the chicken is just cooked through, 1–2 minutes.

Per serving (1 cup): 207 Cal, 6 g Fat, 1 g Sat Fat, 63 mg Chol, 413 mg Sod, 13 g Carb, 1 g Fib, 24 g Prot, 34 mg Calc. **POINTS: 4.**

clever cook's tip

For a quick alternative, substitute ¾ cup of your favorite bottled stir-fry sauce for the liquid ingredients in this recipe. For best results, be sure to marinate the chicken with the cornstarch and 3 tablespoons of the stir-fry sauce for 5 minutes.

Moo Goo Gai Pan

MAKES 4 SERVINGS

A harmonious blend of tender chicken and crunchy vegetables, Moo Goo Gai Pan literally translates as "white mushrooms cooked with sliced chicken."

- 1 **pound skinless boneless chicken thighs, cut into 1-inch pieces**
- 2 **tablespoons cornstarch**
- ½ **cup low-sodium chicken broth**
- 2 **tablespoons reduced-sodium soy sauce**
- 1 **teaspoon Asian (dark) sesame oil**
- 2 **teaspoons canola oil**
- 1 **tablespoon minced peeled fresh ginger**
- 1 **cup canned straw mushrooms, drained**
- ¼ **pound fresh snow peas, trimmed and thinly sliced**
- 1 **red bell pepper, seeded and thinly sliced**
- 3 **scallions, cut into ½-inch pieces**

1. Combine the chicken with 1 tablespoon of the cornstarch in a medium bowl; toss well to coat and set aside. Combine the remaining 1 tablespoon cornstarch, the broth, soy sauce, and sesame oil in a small bowl; set aside.

2. Heat a nonstick wok or a large, deep skillet over medium-high heat until a drop of water sizzles. Swirl in the canola oil, then add the chicken. Stir-fry until lightly browned, 2–3 minutes. Add the ginger and stir-fry until fragrant, about 30 seconds. Add the mushrooms, snow peas, bell pepper, and scallions; stir-fry until crisp-tender, 3–4 minutes. Add the broth mixture and cook, stirring constantly, until the mixture boils and thickens, and the chicken is just cooked through, 1–2 minutes.

Per serving (1¼ cups): 258 Cal, 12 g Fat, 3 g Sat Fat, 77 mg Chol, 558 mg Sod, 11 g Carb, 3 g Fib, 25 g Prot, 37 mg Calc. **POINTS: 6.**

Szechuan Chicken with Peanuts

Szechuan Chicken with Peanuts

MAKES 4 SERVINGS ♦

Dishes from the Szechuan region of China get their spicy kick from hot peppers, such as Szechuan peppercorns, and the liberal use of fresh garlic. Here we use a convenient chili-garlic sauce, but if you want to kick up the heat, add a little Szechuan-style pepper blend (you'll find it in the spice aisle).

- 1 **pound skinless boneless chicken breasts, cut into thin strips**
- 3 **tablespoons hoisin sauce**
- 2 **tablespoons cornstarch**
- ½ **cup low-sodium chicken broth**
- 2 **tablespoons rice vinegar**
- 2 **tablespoons sugar**
- 2 **teaspoons chili-garlic sauce**
- 1 **tablespoon canola oil**
- 1 **tablespoon minced peeled fresh ginger**
- 2 **garlic cloves, minced**
- 1 **green bell pepper, seeded and chopped**
- 2 **medium carrots, thinly sliced on a diagonal**
- ¼ **cup unsalted, dry-roasted peanuts**

1. Combine the chicken, 1 tablespoon of the hoisin sauce, and 1 tablespoon of the cornstarch in a medium bowl; toss well to coat and set aside. Combine the remaining 2 tablespoons hoisin sauce, 1 tablespoon cornstarch, the broth, vinegar, sugar, and chili-garlic sauce in a small bowl; set aside.

2. Heat a nonstick wok or a large, deep skillet over medium-high heat until a drop of water sizzles. Swirl in the oil, then add the chicken. Stir-fry until almost cooked through, 2–3 minutes. Add the ginger and garlic; stir-fry until fragrant, about 15 seconds. Add the bell pepper, carrots, and peanuts; stir-fry until crisp-tender, about 2 minutes. Add the hoisin sauce mixture and cook, stirring constantly, until the mixture boils and thickens, and the chicken is cooked through, about 1 minute.

Per serving (1 cup): 302 Cal, 11 g Fat, 2 g Sat Fat, 64 mg Chol, 392 mg Sod, 24 g Carb, 3 g Fib, 27 g Prot, 38 mg Calc. ***POINTS: 6.***

clever cook's tip

If you don't like peanuts, substitute an equal amount of cashews or your favorite nut.

chinese classics

Chinese Barbecued Pork

MAKES 4 SERVINGS

Reminiscent of the flavor of spare ribs, this glazed pork tenderloin is great served with bok choy stir-fried with a little dark sesame oil, and a hearty bowl of steamed brown rice. Or thinly slice it and serve as an appetizer, with some duck sauce. You can find bottled oyster sauce—a richly flavored brown sauce made from oysters, soy sauce, and brine—in Asian groceries and large supermarkets.

1 (1-pound) boneless pork tenderloin, trimmed of all visible fat
2 tablespoons honey
2 tablespoons hoisin sauce
2 tablespoons sake or dry white wine
2 teaspoons oyster sauce
2 teaspoons reduced-sodium soy sauce
1 teaspoon Asian (dark) sesame oil

1. Prick the tenderloin all over with the tip of a knife or tines of a fork. Combine the honey, hoisin sauce, sake or white wine, oyster sauce, soy sauce, and sesame oil in a large zip-close plastic bag; add the pork. Squeeze out the air and seal the bag; turn to coat the pork. Refrigerate, turning the bag occasionally, at least 6 hours or up to 24 hours.

2. Preheat the oven to 450° F. Spray the rack of a roasting pan with nonstick spray and place in the pan. Remove the tenderloin from the marinade and place on the roasting rack; discard the marinade. Roast until an instant-read thermometer inserted in the thickest part of the tenderloin registers 160° F for medium, 25–27 minutes. Transfer tenderloin to a carving board and let stand 5 minutes before slicing.

Per serving (¼ of tenderloin): 157 Cal, 4 g Fat, 2 g Sat Fat, 67 mg Chol, 110 mg Sod, 3 g Carb, 0 g Fib, 24 g Prot, 6 mg Calc. *POINTS: 3.*

clever cook's tip

Leftover tenderloin, cut into thin strips or diced, makes a terrific addition to your favorite fried rice recipe.

Mu Shu Pork

MAKES 6 SERVINGS

While this classic is one of the most popular dishes in Chinese cuisine, our version reinterprets the meaning of the "pancakes." Chinese cabbage lends a delicate flavor and texture to this dish. Long and pale green, it is not as strongly flavored as our common green cabbage or savoy cabbage.

- 1 **pound boneless pork tenderloin, trimmed of all visible fat, cut into thin strips**
- 6 **tablespoons dry sherry**
- 2 **tablespoons + 2 teaspoons reduced-sodium soy sauce**
- 1 **tablespoon + 1 teaspoon cornstarch**
- ½ **teaspoon Asian (dark) sesame oil**
- ¼ **cup hoisin sauce**
- 6 **(6-inch) flour tortillas**
- 1 **tablespoon canola oil**
- ¼ **pound shiitake mushrooms, stemmed and thinly sliced**
- 2 **tablespoons minced peeled fresh ginger**
- 3 **garlic cloves, minced**
- ¾ **pound Chinese cabbage, thinly sliced**
- 6 **scallions, chopped**

1. Combine the pork, 2 tablespoons of the sherry, 2 teaspoons soy sauce, 1 tablespoon cornstarch, and the sesame oil in a medium bowl; toss well to coat and set aside. Combine the remaining 4 tablespoons sherry, 2 tablespoons soy sauce, and 1 teaspoon cornstarch with the hoisin sauce in a small bowl; set aside.

2. Stack the tortillas on a microwaveproof plate. Cover with plastic wrap and microwave on High 1 minute; set aside and keep warm.

3. Heat a nonstick wok or a large, deep skillet over medium-high heat until a drop of water sizzles. Swirl in 2 teaspoons of the canola oil, then add the pork mixture. Stir-fry until just cooked through, 4–5 minutes; transfer to a plate. Swirl the remaining 1 teaspoon canola oil, then add the mushrooms, ginger, and garlic. Stir-fry until softened, 3–4 minutes. Add the cabbage and 2 tablespoons water; stir-fry until the cabbage wilts and is crisp-tender, 2–3 minutes. Add the scallions, pork, and sherry mixture. Cook, stirring constantly, until the mixture boils and thickens, about 1 minute. Spoon about ⅔ cup of the pork mixture onto each tortilla, roll up, and serve.

Per serving (1 roll): 272 Cal, 9 g Fat, 1 g Sat Fat, 45 mg Chol, 716 mg Sod, 27 g Carb, 3 g Fib, 22 g Prot, 69 mg Calc. **POINTS: 6.**

clever cook's tip

This dish is great the next day. Just prepare the pork filling, cool to room temperature, then refrigerate, covered. When ready to serve, spray a large nonstick skillet with nonstick spray and set over medium-high heat. Add the pork mixture and cook until heated through.

Singapore Chow Mai Fun

MAKES 4 SERVINGS 🔥

Mai fun are thin rice noodles, or rice vermicelli. They can usually be found in larger supermarkets in the Asian foods section. Unlike noodles made from wheat, rice noodles are rarely boiled; instead, they are soaked in hot water until they soften.

6 ounces mai fun (rice sticks or rice noodles)

½ cup low-sodium chicken broth

3 tablespoons reduced-sodium soy sauce

1 tablespoon rice vinegar

2 teaspoons chili-garlic sauce

1 teaspoon sugar

6 ounces lean ground pork (10% or less fat)

1 onion, chopped

3 garlic cloves, minced

2 tablespoons curry powder

1 red bell pepper, seeded and finely chopped

1. Bring a large pot of water to a boil. Remove from the heat; add the mai fun and soak until softened, 5–6 minutes. Drain and set aside.

2. Combine the broth, soy sauce, vinegar, chili-garlic sauce, and sugar in a small bowl; set aside.

3. Spray a nonstick wok or a large, deep skillet with nonstick spray and set over medium-high heat. Add the pork and stir-fry until just cooked through, about 3 minutes. Add the onion, garlic, and curry powder. Stir-fry until softened and fragrant, about 3 minutes. Add the bell pepper and stir-fry until crisp-tender, about 2 minutes. Add the broth mixture and cook, stirring constantly, until the mixture boils and thickens, about 1 minute. Add the noodles and cook until heated through, about 1 minute.

Per serving (1½ cups): 265 Cal, 2 g Fat, 1 g Sat Fat, 26 mg Chol, 595 mg Sod, 45 g Carb, 4 g Fib, 15 g Prot, 55 mg Calc. *POINTS: 5.*

clever cook's tip

For a vegetarian version, substitute ½ pound extra-firm low-fat tofu, cubed, for the pork, and vegetable broth for the chicken broth. Add the tofu with the bell pepper.

Sweet-and-Sour Pork

MAKES 4 SERVINGS

The sauce in this dish is extremely versatile. Try substituting chicken, shrimp, scallops, or even skinless duck breasts for the pork in this recipe.

1 **pound pork tenderloin, trimmed of all visible fat, cut into ½-inch cubes**
2 **tablespoons cornstarch**
⅓ **cup water**
¼ **cup rice vinegar**
¼ **cup sugar**
3 **tablespoons ketchup**
2 **tablespoons reduced-sodium soy sauce**
1 **tablespoon canola oil**
1 **tablespoon minced peeled fresh ginger**
2 **garlic cloves, minced**
1 **green bell pepper, seeded and cut into ½-inch pieces**
1 **(8-ounce) can pineapple chunks in juice, drained**

1. Combine the pork with 1 tablespoon of the cornstarch in a medium bowl; toss well to coat and set aside. Combine the remaining 1 tablespoon cornstarch, the water, vinegar, sugar, ketchup, and soy sauce in a small bowl; set aside.

2. Heat a nonstick wok or a large, deep skillet over medium-high heat until a drop of water sizzles. Swirl in the oil, then add the pork. Stir-fry until almost cooked through, 2–3 minutes. Add the ginger and garlic. Stir-fry until fragrant, about 30 seconds. Add the bell pepper and pineapple; stir-fry until crisp-tender, about 3 minutes. Add the vinegar mixture and cook, stirring constantly, until the mixture boils and thickens and the pork is just cooked through, 1–2 minutes.

Per serving (1 cup): 287 Cal, 8 g Fat, 2 g Sat Fat, 67 mg Chol, 488 mg Sod, 29 g Carb, 1 g Fib, 25 g Prot, 19 mg Calc. *POINTS: 6.*

Beef Lo Mein

MAKES 6 SERVINGS

A Chinese custom for formal dinners is to serve a dish made with mein (noodles). A dish with long mein signifies long life. Sake (Japanese rice wine) adds wonderful depth of flavor to this beef and noodle dish.

½ **pound fresh lo mein noodles or spaghetti**

¾ **cup low-sodium beef broth**

¼ **cup sake or rice wine**

¼ **cup reduced-sodium soy sauce**

1½ **tablespoons cornstarch**

1 **tablespoon sugar**

1 **teaspoon Asian (dark) sesame oil**

1 **tablespoon canola oil**

¾ **pound beef top round, trimmed of all visible fat, cut into thin strips**

½ **pound white mushrooms, sliced**

3 **scallions, chopped**

3 **garlic cloves, minced**

1. Cook the noodles or spaghetti according to package directions; drain and set aside. Combine the broth, sake or rice wine, soy sauce, cornstarch, sugar, and sesame oil in a small bowl; set aside.

2. Heat a nonstick wok or a large, deep skillet over medium-high heat until a drop of water sizzles. Swirl in 2 teaspoons of the canola oil, then add the beef. Stir-fry until just cooked through, 3–4 minutes; transfer to a plate. Swirl in the remaining 1 teaspoon canola oil, then add the mushrooms, scallions, and garlic. Stir-fry until softened, about 3 minutes. Add the broth mixture and cook, stirring constantly, until the mixture boils and thickens, about 2 minutes. Stir in the beef and noodles. Cook, tossing frequently, until heated through, about 1 minute.

Per serving (1 cup): 290 Cal, 6 g Fat, 1 g Sat Fat, 35 mg Chol, 442 mg Sod, 37 g Carb, 2 g Fib, 20 g Prot, 20 mg Calc. *POINTS: 6.*

clever cook's tip

Nonstick woks, stir-fry pans, and large, deep skillets all work well for health-conscious cooks because they eliminate the need for excessive amounts of oil. A traditional iron wok should periodically be seasoned by lightly coating the pan with vegetable oil and heating over low heat until hot. Woks can be washed with liquid detergent and a soft scrubber as long as it is dried well after cleaning and not allowed to rust.

Beef with Broccoli

MAKES 4 SERVINGS

Dishes made with broccoli are a Chinese-takeout favorite, perhaps because broccoli is so perfect for absorbing flavors from the sauce. Here's a traditional recipe that you can make almost as fast as you can order it. To save even more time, buy lean beef round steak precut into strips and stock up on precut broccoli florets from your supermarket's salad bar.

- ¾ **pound beef top round, trimmed of all visible fat, cut into thin strips**
- 2 **tablespoons cornstarch**
- ½ **cup low-sodium beef broth**
- 2 **tablespoons oyster sauce**
- 2 **tablespoons honey**
- 2 **tablespoons reduced-sodium soy sauce**
- 1 **tablespoon dry sherry**
- 1 **pound broccoli crowns, cut into florets (4 cups)**
- 2 **teaspoons canola oil**
- 1 **tablespoon minced peeled fresh ginger**
- 3 **garlic cloves, minced**

1. Combine the beef with 1 tablespoon of the cornstarch; toss well to coat and set aside. Combine the remaining 1 tablespoon cornstarch, the broth, oyster sauce, honey, soy sauce and sherry in a small bowl; set aside.

2. Bring a large pot of water to a boil; add the broccoli and cook until crisp-tender, 3–4 minutes; drain.

3. Heat a nonstick wok or a large, deep skillet over medium-high heat until a drop of water sizzles. Swirl in the oil, then add the beef. Stir-fry until just cooked through, 3–4 minutes; transfer to a plate.

4. Add the ginger and garlic to the wok and stir-fry until fragrant, about 20 seconds. Add the broth mixture and cook, stirring constantly, until the mixture boils and thickens, about 1 minute. Add the beef and broccoli and cook until heated through, about 1 minute.

Per serving (1 cup): 216 Cal, 6 g Fat, 1 g Sat Fat, 53 mg Chol, 425 mg Sod, 18 g Carb, 2 g Fib, 23 g Prot, 45 mg Calc. *POINTS: 4.*

clever cook's tip

If you prefer you can use peanut oil instead of canola oil. Peanut oil is prized for its high smoke point, which makes it good for frying foods at high temperatures. For a distinctive peanut flavor, choose Chinese peanut oil over the blander American counterpart.

Spicy Orange Beef
with Vegetables

Spicy Orange Beef with Vegetables

MAKES 4 SERVINGS 🔥

While this dish is strictly Asian in design, it also works wonderfully as an East-meets-West fajita. For an Asian meal, serve with rice and garnish with fresh orange segments. For a Western meal, serve in warmed flour tortillas.

¾ **pound beef top round, trimmed of all visible fat, cut into thin strips**

2 **tablespoons cornstarch**

2 **teaspoons grated orange rind**

½ **cup low-sodium beef broth**

¼ **cup orange juice**

2 **tablespoons reduced-sodium soy sauce**

1 **tablespoon sugar**

1½ **teaspoons chili-garlic sauce or ¼ teaspoon crushed red pepper**

4 **teaspoons canola oil**

1 **tablespoon minced peeled fresh ginger**

¼ **pound green beans, halved crosswise**

1 **red bell pepper, seeded and cut into thin strips**

1 **carrot, cut into matchstick-thin strips**

1. Combine the beef, 1 tablespoon of the cornstarch, and the orange rind in a medium bowl; toss well to coat and set aside. Combine the remaining 1 tablespoon cornstarch, the broth, orange juice, soy sauce, sugar, and chili-garlic sauce or crushed red pepper in a small bowl; set aside.

2. Heat a nonstick wok or a large, deep skillet over medium-high heat until a drop of water sizzles. Swirl in 2 teaspoons of the oil, then add the beef. Stir-fry until cooked through, 2–3 minutes; transfer to a plate. Swirl the remaining 2 teaspoons oil, then add the ginger. Stir-fry until fragrant, about 10 seconds. Add the green beans, bell pepper, and carrot. Stir-fry until crisp-tender, 2–3 minutes. Add the broth mixture and cook, stirring constantly, until the mixture boils and thickens, about 1 minute. Add the beef and cook until hot, about 1 minute.

Per serving (1 cup): 227 Cal, 8 g Fat, 2 g Sat Fat, 53 mg Chol, 441 mg Sod, 16 g Carb, 2 g Fib, 22 g Prot, 29 mg Calc. *POINTS: 5.*

Mango and Green Tea Sorbet

MAKES 6 SERVINGS

Green tea can be found in most markets that sell Asian ingredients and at many large supermarkets. If you can't find loose green tea, just cut open a few green tea bags to get the amount you need.

1 cup water
½ cup green tea leaves
½ cup sugar
3 ripe mangoes, peeled, seeded, and coarsely chopped
1 tablespoon fresh lemon juice

1. Combine the water and tea leaves in a small saucepan. Bring just to a boil, then remove from the heat and let brew 5 minutes. Strain, discarding the leaves, and return the tea to the saucepan. Add the sugar; bring to a boil. Boil until the sugar dissolves, about 1 minute. Remove from the heat and cool completely, about 30 minutes.

2. Puree the mangos, lemon juice, and ⅔ cup of the tea mixture in a food processor. Pour into an 8-inch square baking pan and freeze about 3 hours.

3. Transfer the frozen mango mixture to a food processor. Pulse the mixture until smooth, 30–40 seconds. Serve at once or store in the freezer for up to 2 months. Soften 10 minutes before serving.

Per serving (scant ½ cup): 133 Cal, 0 g Fat, 0 g Sat Fat, 0 mg Chol, 2 mg Sod, 35 g Carb, 2 g Fib, 1 g Prot, 11 mg Calc. *POINTS: 2.*

clever cook's tip

To help speed up this recipe, cool the mango-tea mixture over a bowl of ice water, stirring often, about 10 minutes. This will also help to quicken the freezing time.

the perfect pantry

Here, a list of the necessary ingredients to have on hand when cooking the Chinese way.

- **Bamboo shoots:** Tender-crisp ivory shoot of an edible species of bamboo plant.
- **Black bean sauce:** Savory, ready-to-use sauce with fermented black beans.
- **Bok choy:** Mild-tasting vegetable with crunchy white stalks and tender dark green leaves.
- **Chili-garlic sauce:** Sauce made from hot peppers, salt, and garlic.
- **Chinese cabbage:** Mild-tasting cabbage with crisp, crinkly, thin leaves.
- **Chinese rice vinegar:** Vinegar made from fermented rice, is slightly milder than Western vinegar; three varieties: white (clear or pale amber), red, and black; white is most commonly used.
- **Chinese rice wine:** A sweet, golden wine made from fermenting steamed glutinous rice.
- **Chow mein noodles:** Wheat flour noodles; for chow mein dishes stir-fried ingredients are served over noodles that have been cooked separately.
- **Ginger:** Knobby tan root; flesh varies in color from pale greenish yellow to ivory; peppery and slightly sweet flavor; pungent, spicy aroma.
- **Green tea:** Greenish-yellow tea with a slightly bitter flavor.
- **Hoisin sauce:** Thick, reddish-brown sauce made from a mixture of soybeans, garlic, chiles, and spices; sweet-spicy flavor.
- **Lo mein noodles:** Wheat flour noodles similar to chow mein; for lo mein dishes boiled noodles are tossed in the wok with other ingredients during the final stages of cooking.
- **Mai fun (rice sticks or rice noodles):** Variety of thin rice noodles.
- **Oyster sauce:** Thick, dark brown sauce made from cooked oysters, brine, and soy sauce.
- **Sake:** Japanese wine made from fermented rice; yellowish in color, slightly sweet flavor.
- **Sesame oil:** Oil pressed from sesame seeds; two basic types: light sesame oil with delicate taste and Asian (dark) sesame oil, which has a much stronger flavor and fragrance and is more commonly used in Asian and Indian cuisine.
- **Shiitake mushrooms:** Variety of mushroom with dark brown caps, tough, thin stems, and meaty flesh with full-bodied woodsy flavor.
- **Snow peas:** Delicate, thin legume with bright green edible pod; seeds inside are tender and sweet.
- **Soy sauce:** Dark, salty sauce made by fermenting boiled soybeans and roasted wheat or barley; we prefer reduced-sodium soy sauce.
- **Straw mushrooms:** Tiny, earthy-tasting mushrooms; color ranges from pale tan when young to dark charcoal gray when mature; mostly available canned.
- **Szechuan pepper:** Mildly hot spice native to the Szechuan province of China; comes from the prickly ash tree.
- **Tofu:** Soy milk curd drained and pressed into cakes.
- **Water chestnuts:** Crunchy, juicy edible tuber of a water plant indigenous to Southeast Asia; bland with a hint of sweetness; mostly available canned.
- **Wonton wrappers:** Paper-thin sheets of dough made from flour, eggs, and salt; available in both squares and circles.
- **Wood-ear mushrooms:** Delicate, neutral-flavored mushroom sold fresh or dried; dried resemble brownish-black dried chips.

chinese classics

3

greek diner delights

Avgolemono Soup

This creamy, tangy chicken soup is a simple combination of eggs, fresh lemon juice, and rice. It is wonderful served with pita bread for a simple lunch or as an accompaniment to our Spanakopita [page 64]. For a heartier version (and an extra 1 **POINT** per serving), stir in 4 ounces cooked shredded chicken just before serving.

5 cups low-sodium, fat-free chicken broth

6 tablespoons long-grain white rice

3 large eggs

¼ cup fresh lemon juice

⅛ teaspoon freshly ground pepper

1. In a large saucepan, bring the broth to a boil over medium-high heat. Add the rice; reduce heat to medium-low and simmer, covered, 20 minutes.

2. Meanwhile, combine the eggs, lemon juice, and pepper in a medium bowl; whisk until frothy. Gradually add 2 cups of the hot broth, whisking constantly to keep the egg mixture from curdling. Pour the egg mixture into the saucepan and cook, stirring constantly, 1 minute longer. Serve at once.

Per serving (1⅓ cups): 142 Cal, 4 g Fat, 1 g Sat Fat, 159 mg Chol, 848 mg Sod, 18 g Carb, 0 g Fib, 7 g Prot, 25 mg Calc. **POINTS: 3.**

the perfect pantry

Stock these Mediterranean must-have ingredients if you're looking for authentic Greek flavor.

- **Cinnamon:** Spice often used in tomato and meat sauces, stews, pies, and desserts.
- **Dill:** Herb used in pies, stuffing, sauces, and salads; mostly used fresh.
- **Extra-virgin olive oil:** Oil produced from first pressing of olives; low acidity; rich, deep, olive flavor; color can range from greenish golden to bright green.
- **Feta cheese:** Cured cheese made of sheep's, goat's, or cow's milk; white, crumbly, and rindless; available crumbled and in square cakes; rich, tangy flavor.
- **Honey:** Mostly used in sweets and desserts; use lighter varieties such as orange-blossom honey.
- **Kalamata olives:** Dark purple, almond-shaped Greek olive; rich and fruity flavor; packed in olive oil or vinegar.
- **Oregano:** Herb commonly used fresh or dried in salads, sauces, and roasted fish; often found in the company of garlic and lemon.
- **Orzo:** Tiny, rice-shaped pasta.
- **Mint:** Herb often used fresh or dried in savory and sweet rice stuffing and cheese pies.
- **Phyllo dough:** Ultrathin sheets of pastry dough; available fresh or frozen.
- **Pita bread:** Middle Eastern flat bread made of white or whole-wheat flour.
- **Tahini:** Thick paste made of ground sesame seeds.

Greek Villagers' Salad

MAKES 4 SERVINGS

A classic combination of chunky vegetables, pepperoncini, olives, feta cheese, and oregano that is tossed with vinaigrette dressing. Do this salad justice by selecting the ripest tomatoes you can find. Serve with toasted flat breads for a light lunch.

- **3 ripe tomatoes, cut into 6 wedges each**
- **2 green bell peppers, seeded and cut into rings**
- **1 cucumber, peeled and cut into ¼-inch-thick slices**
- **4 pepperoncini**
- **½ cup sliced red onion**
- **6 kalamata olives, pitted and halved**
- **2 tablespoons red-wine vinegar**
- **1 tablespoon extra-virgin olive oil**
- **1 teaspoon dried oregano**
- **⅛ teaspoon salt**
- **⅛ teaspoon freshly ground pepper**
- **2 ounces reduced-fat feta cheese, crumbled (about ½ cup)**
- **2 pita breads, toasted and cut in half crosswise**

Combine the tomatoes, bell peppers, cucumber, pepperoncini, onion, olives, vinegar, oil, oregano, salt, and pepper in a large serving bowl; toss well. Sprinkle salad with the feta. Serve with pita breads.

Per serving (¼ of salad with ½ pita bread): 215 Cal, 8 g Fat, 2 g Sat Fat, 5 mg Chol, 534 mg Sod, 31 g Carb, 4 g Fib, 8 g Prot, 96 mg Calc. *POINTS: 4.*

clever cook's tip

Pepperoncini are small peppers packed in vinegar that can be found in most supermarkets.

greek diner delights

Hummus

MAKES 10 SERVINGS

Thanks to the food processor and the convenience of canned chickpeas, making your own hummus (chickpea puree) takes only minutes and yields great taste as well as impressive nutritional dividends. Our dip is just as rich and creamy as the original but uses only a fraction of the high-fat tahini (sesame paste). Serve with toasted pita chips or bread, or use as a spread for vegetable wraps.

1 (15½-ounce) can chickpeas (garbanzo beans)
4 teaspoons tahini
1 tablespoon fresh lemon juice
1 teaspoon grated lemon rind
1 clove garlic
⅛ teaspoon ground cumin
⅛ teaspoon salt

1. Drain and rinse chickpeas, reserving ⅓ cup of the canned chickpea liquid; set aside.

2. In a food processor or blender, combine the chickpeas, tahini, lemon juice, lemon rind, garlic, cumin, and salt. With the processor running, gradually add the reserved chickpea liquid through the feed tube and process until smooth.

Per serving (¼ cup): 63 Cal, 2 g Fat, 0 g Sat Fat, 0 mg Chol, 192 mg Sod, 8 g Carb, 2 g Fib, 3 g Prot, 23 mg Calc. *POINTS: 1.*

clever cook's tip

If you don't have tahini on hand or forget to buy it, you can substitute an equal amount of natural peanut butter—just be sure to use the smooth kind.

Tzatziki

MAKES 10 SERVINGS

This garlicky cucumber-yogurt sauce is a mainstay of Greek cuisine. Tzatziki may be served as a vegetable dip, with crackers, or as a condiment to our Lamb Souvlaki with Rice [page 73]. The yogurt needs to drain at least several hours until thick and creamy for this recipe, so plan ahead.

- 2 cups yogurt cheese*
- 1 cucumber, peeled, seeded, grated, and squeezed dry
- 2 cloves garlic, minced
- 4 teaspoons extra-virgin olive oil
- 1 tablespoon chopped fresh dill
- 1 tablespoon fresh lemon juice
- ½ teaspoon salt

Combine the yogurt cheese, cucumber, garlic, oil, dill, lemon juice, and salt in a bowl; mix well.

*To make 2 cups yogurt cheese, spoon 1 (32-ounce) container plain nonfat yogurt into a coffee filter or a cheesecloth-lined strainer; set over a bowl and let stand in the refrigerator 2 hours or overnight. Discard the liquid.

Per serving (¼ cup): 70 Cal, 2 g Fat, 0 g Sat Fat, 2 mg Chol, 186 mg Sod, 8 g Carb, 0 g Fib, 5 g Prot, 185 mg Calc. *POINTS: 2.*

clever cook's tip

Surprisingly, the flavors of Tzatziki improve with time. Try refrigerating it a day or two before serving so that the ingredients have a chance to blend.

Spanakopita

This spinach pie is typically served in a single dish and cut into wedges, but we've prepared individual phyllo triangles, which can be served as either an appetizer or as an entrée. For a Southwestern twist, try substituting queso blanco or low-fat Monterey Jack cheese for the feta cheese and chopped fresh cilantro for the dill.

1 teaspoon extra-virgin olive oil
1 onion, finely chopped
1 (16-ounce) bag frozen chopped spinach, thawed and squeezed dry
4 ounces reduced-fat feta cheese, crumbled (about 1 cup)
⅓ cup chopped fresh dill
⅓ cup chopped fresh parsley
1 large egg, lightly beaten
⅛ teaspoon ground nutmeg
⅛ teaspoon salt
⅛ teaspoon freshly ground pepper
8 (12 x 17-inch) sheets phyllo dough, thawed according to package directions if frozen

1. Preheat oven to 350° F. Spray a large baking sheet with nonstick spray; set aside.

2. To make the filling, heat a large nonstick skillet over medium-high heat. Swirl in the oil, then add the onion. Cook until softened, 4–5 minutes. Add the spinach and cook 3–4 minutes. Remove from the heat; cool 5 minutes. Stir in the feta, dill, parsley, egg, nutmeg, salt, and pepper; mix well to combine.

3. Place one sheet of phyllo with the long side facing you on a work surface (cover remaining phyllo with plastic wrap to retain moisture). Lightly spray the phyllo sheet with nonstick spray; top with a second phyllo sheet and lightly spray with nonstick spray. With a sharp knife, cut the layered sheets crosswise into 3 equal strips.

4. Place a scant ⅓ cup of the filling in the center of the bottom end of one strip. Fold up one corner around filling to form a triangle (flag-style). Continue folding all the way up to the top of the strip. Place the triangle, seam-side down, on the baking sheet. Repeat with the other 2 strips, then with the remaining phyllo sheets, nonstick spray, and filling to make 12 triangles.

5. Bake triangles until lightly golden, 20–25 minutes. Serve warm or at room temperature.

Per serving (2 triangles): 161 Cal, 6 g Fat, 2 g Sat Fat, 42 mg Chol, 490 mg Sod, 19 g Carb, 3 g Fib, 9 g Prot, 145 mg Calc. *POINTS: 3.*

clever cook's tip

These spanakopita triangles freeze beautifully. Prepare as directed through Step 3. Freeze triangles on a baking sheet in a single layer, then transfer the frozen triangles to zip-close plastic bags; seal and freeze for up to 3 weeks. To serve, do not thaw. Bake as directed in Step 4, except increase the baking time to 27 to 35 minutes.

Savory Squash Pie

MAKES 4 SERVINGS

Pittas, or pies, are to the Greeks what pasta is to the Italians—the ultimate comfort food. Kolokithopita, or squash pie, is a seasonal classic in northern Greece and is traditionally made with zucchini, rice, feta cheese, and fresh herbs. But it can also be prepared with pumpkin, yellow squash, or any combination of your favorite squashes.

1 tablespoon extra-virgin olive oil
1 onion, chopped
1½ pounds zucchini, trimmed, grated, and squeezed dry
1½ cups cooked white rice
3 ounces reduced-fat feta cheese, crumbled (about ¾ cup)
⅓ cup chopped fresh mint
⅓ cup chopped fresh parsley
1 large egg, lightly beaten
¼ teaspoon salt
⅛ teaspoon freshly ground pepper
6 (12 x 17-inch) sheets phyllo dough, thawed according to package directions if frozen

1. Preheat oven to 350° F. Spray a 7 x 11-inch baking dish with nonstick spray; set aside.

2. To make the filling, heat a large nonstick skillet over medium-high heat. Swirl in 1 teaspoon of the oil, then add the onion. Cook until softened, 4–5 minutes; transfer to a bowl. Swirl the remaining 2 teaspoons oil into the same skillet, then add the zucchini. Cook until the liquid from the zucchini evaporates, 8–10 minutes. Transfer zucchini to the bowl with the onions. Add the rice, feta, mint, parsley, egg, salt, and pepper; mix well to combine.

3. Place one sheet of phyllo with the long side facing you on a work surface (cover remaining phyllo with plastic wrap to retain moisture). Lightly spray the phyllo sheet with nonstick spray; top with a second phyllo sheet and lightly spray with nonstick spray. Repeat with the remaining phyllo sheets to form a stack. With a sharp knife, cut the layered sheets crosswise in half. Place one-half of the phyllo in the bottom of the baking pan. Spread top with the filling, then cover filling with the remaining half of the phyllo sheets. Bake until the phyllo is golden and the filling is hot, 30 minutes.

Per serving (¼ of pie): 299 Cal, 10 g Fat, 3 g Sat Fat, 61 mg Chol, 606 mg Sod, 42 g Carb, 4 g Fib, 12 g Prot, 124 mg Calc. *POINTS: 6*

clever cook's tip

Thaw frozen phyllo overnight in the refrigerator. Once opened, keep phyllo refrigerated and tightly wrapped up to 3 days. Phyllo will become brittle if refrozen.

greek diner delights

Pastitsio

MAKES 8 SERVINGS

This baked pasta casserole is probably one of the most recognizable Greek dishes on restaurant menus. (Moussaka is a similar dish but substitutes sliced eggplant for the pasta.) Serve Pastitsio with a salad of tossed greens, chopped scallions, fresh fennel, and fresh dill.

3 cups reduced-fat (2%) milk

¼ cup cornstarch

3 large eggs, lightly beaten

8 tablespoons grated Parmesan cheese

¾ teaspoon salt

¼ teaspoon freshly ground pepper

⅛ teaspoon ground nutmeg

½ pound spaghetti

1 tablespoon extra-virgin olive oil

1 onion, chopped

¾ pound lean ground sirloin (10% or less fat)

1 pound plum tomatoes, chopped (about 2 cups)

2 garlic cloves, minced

¾ teaspoon ground cinnamon

1. Preheat oven to 350° F. Spray a 7 x 11-inch baking dish with nonstick spray; set aside.

2. To make the white sauce, combine the milk, cornstarch, and eggs in a large saucepan. Cook over low heat, stirring constantly, until thickened, 7–9 minutes. Remove from the heat and stir in 6 tablespoons of the Parmesan, ¼ teaspoon of the salt, ⅛ teaspoon of the pepper, and the nutmeg; cover and set aside.

3. Bring a large pot of lightly salted water to a boil. Add spaghetti and cook according to package directions. Drain and set aside.

4. To make the filling, heat a large nonstick skillet over medium-high heat. Swirl in the oil, then add the onion. Cook, stirring occasionally, until the onion is softened, 4–6 minutes. Add the sirloin and cook, breaking up the meat with a wooden spoon, until browned, 5–6 minutes. Stir in the tomatoes, garlic, cinnamon, and the remaining ½ teaspoon salt and ⅛ teaspoon pepper. Cook, stirring often, until liquid from the tomatoes evaporates, 4–5 minutes.

5. Arrange half of the cooked spaghetti in an even layer on the bottom of the baking pan. Top with the filling, then top with the remaining spaghetti. Spread the white sauce evenly over the spaghetti. Sprinkle sauce with the remaining 2 tablespoons cheese. Bake until top is golden, 30–35 minutes. Cool at least 5 minutes before serving.

Per serving (1 cup): 319 Cal, 11 g Fat, 4 g Sat Fat, 103 mg Chol, 512 mg Sod, 36 g Carb, 3 g Fib, 19 g Prot, 226 mg Calc. *POINTS: 7.*

Pastitsio

Baked Orzo with Fragrant Lamb

Throughout Greece and the Mediterranean, meat is thought of as a condiment, rather than the primary ingredient of an entrée. Since the lamb simmers in a highly seasoned tomato sauce in this recipe, it takes a mere 6 ounces to give the dish its rich, meaty flavor. You can easily substitute lean ground beef for the lamb, if desired.

½ **pound orzo**

6 **ounces lean ground lamb (10% or less fat)**

1 **onion, chopped**

¼ **cup chopped fennel bulb**

2 **cloves garlic, minced**

1 **teaspoon dried mint**

½ **teaspoon dried oregano**

1 **(14-ounce) can crushed tomatoes**

3 **tablespoons tomato paste**

½ **teaspoon ground cinnamon**

3 **ounces reduced-fat feta cheese, crumbled (about ¾ cup)**

2 **tablespoons grated Parmesan cheese**

1. Preheat oven to 350° F. Spray an 8-inch square baking dish with nonstick spray; set aside.

2. Bring a large pot of salted water to a boil. Add the orzo and cook according to package directions. Drain and transfer to a large bowl.

3. Heat a large nonstick skillet over medium-high heat. Add the lamb and cook, stirring to break up the meat with a wooden spoon, until browned, 3–4 minutes. Remove lamb with a slotted spoon and transfer to the bowl with the orzo.

4. Add the onion, fennel, garlic, mint, and oregano to the same skillet. Cook, stirring, until onion begins to soften, 3–4 minutes. Add the tomatoes, tomato paste, and cinnamon; cook until mixture thickens, 6–8 minutes.

5. Combine the tomato mixture with the orzo and lamb. Stir in the feta and mix well. Pour mixture into the baking pan. Sprinkle top with the Parmesan. Bake until hot, 25 minutes.

Per serving (1¼ cups): 286 Cal, 6 g Fat, 3 g Sat Fat, 37 mg Chol, 354 mg Sod, 38 g Carb, 3 g Fib, 20 g Prot, 117 mg Calc. **POINTS: 6.**

Dolmades with Lemon-Egg Sauce

MAKES 6 SERVINGS

Dolmades, which means something stuffed, are savory little packages filled with fruits, vegetables, rice, or meats alone or in any combination. Grape and cabbage leaves are the most common wrappers. In this recipe we chose green cabbage leaves with a lamb, rice, and herb stuffing.

- 1 **head green cabbage**
- 6 **ounces lean ground lamb (10% or less fat)**
- 1 **onion, chopped**
- ¾ **cup long-grain white rice**
- 2 **cloves garlic, minced**
- 3 **tablespoons chopped fresh dill**
- 3 **tablespoons chopped fresh parsley**
- 2 **tablespoons tomato paste**
- 1 **teaspoon dried oregano**
- ¾ **teaspoon salt**
- ¼ **teaspoon freshly ground pepper**
- 2 **large eggs**
- 6 **tablespoons fresh lemon juice**

1. Bring a large pot of lightly salted water to a boil. Add the cabbage and cook 4 minutes; drain. When the cabbage is cool enough to handle, remove 12 whole outer leaves. Wipe out pot, spray bottom with nonstick spray, and set both aside.

2. Heat a large nonstick skillet over medium-high heat. Add the lamb and cook, stirring to break up the meat with a wooden spoon, until browned, 3–4 minutes. Add the onion, rice, and garlic; cook 4 minutes. Stir in the dill, parsley, tomato paste, oregano, ½ teaspoon of the salt, and ⅛ teaspoon of the pepper; cook 2 minutes. Add 1 cup water, cover skillet, and reduce the heat to medium-low. Simmer mixture 15 minutes (the rice will not be fully cooked). Cool 10 minutes.

3. Working 1 cabbage leaf at a time, place ¼ cup of the filling in the center of the bottom third of the leaf. Fold over sides, then roll up from the bottom to form a package. Place roll, seam-side down, in the pot. Repeat with remaining cabbage leaves and filling.

4. Add enough water to come 2 inches up the side of the pot; bring to a boil. Cover pot, reduce heat to medium-low and simmer, until dolmades are tender and rice is cooked through, 1½ hours. Transfer dolmades with a slotted spoon to a serving platter. Transfer 1 cup of the cooking liquid to a saucepan. Cover dolmades with foil and keep warm.

5. Combine the eggs, lemon juice, and the remaining ¼ teaspoon salt and ⅛ teaspoon pepper in a bowl; whisk until frothy. Bring the reserved cooking liquid to a boil. Gradually add the hot liquid, whisking constantly to keep the egg mixture from curdling. Pour the egg mixture into the saucepan and cook, stirring constantly over low heat, 1 minute longer. Pour sauce over the dolmades and serve at once.

Per serving (2 dolmades with 2 tablespoons sauce): 196 Cal, 4 g Fat, 1 g Sat Fat, 94 mg Chol, 336 mg Sod, 28 g Carb, 2 g Fib, 13 g Prot, 51 mg Calc. **POINTS: 4.**

Greek Meatballs

Keftedakia, miniature beef meatballs, are a favorite finger food in Greece. Traditionally these meatballs are deep-fried, but we've opted for a healthier take by substituting highly seasoned ground turkey for the beef and simmering the meatballs in a hearty tomato sauce. A side of orzo rounds out the meal.

¾ **pound skinless ground turkey**

1 **cup chopped onion**

⅓ **cup plain dried bread crumbs**

4 **cloves garlic, minced**

1 **large egg**

¼ **cup grated Parmesan cheese**

3 **tablespoons chopped fresh parsley**

1 **tablespoon chopped fresh mint**

2 **teaspoons dried oregano**

½ **teaspoon ground cinnamon**

1 **tablespoon extra-virgin olive oil**

1 **(28-ounce) can whole peeled tomatoes, chopped**

3 **tablespoons tomato paste**

¼ **teaspoon salt**

½ **pound orzo, cooked according to package directions**

1. Preheat oven to 400° F. Spray a large jelly-roll pan with nonstick spray; set aside.

2. To make the meatballs, combine the turkey, ½ cup of the onion, bread crumbs, half the minced garlic, egg, Parmesan, parsley, mint, 1 teaspoon of the oregano, and ¼ teaspoon of the cinnamon in a large bowl; mix well. With damp hands, form into 18 (1-inch) meatballs. Place meatballs on baking sheet and bake, turning once, 20 minutes. Set aside.

3. Meanwhile, heat a large saucepan over medium-high heat. Swirl in the oil, then add the remaining ½ cup onion, minced garlic, and 1 teaspoon oregano. Cook until onion softens, 2 minutes. Add the tomatoes, tomato paste, salt, and the remaining ¼ teaspoon cinnamon; bring to a boil. Reduce heat to low and cook, stirring occasionally, until sauce begins to thicken slightly, 15 minutes. Add the meatballs and simmer 15 minutes longer.

4. Divide orzo among six serving bowls. Top each serving with sauce and meatballs.

Per serving (3 meatballs with ½ cup orzo): 327 Cal, 9 g Fat, 3 g Sat Fat, 72 mg Chol, 482 mg Sod, 44 g Carb, 4 g Fib, 18 g Prot, 151 mg Calc. *POINTS: 6.*

Lemon–Garlic Roast Chicken

MAKES 4 SERVINGS

This taverna-style chicken is usually prepared with the whole bird, but to save time (without skimping on flavor) we opted for using skinless bone-in chicken breasts and roasting them on a bed of potatoes.

¼ cup fresh lemon juice

1½ tablespoons extra-virgin olive oil

3 cloves garlic, minced

1 teaspoon dried oregano

½ teaspoon dried marjoram

¾ teaspoon salt

¼ teaspoon freshly ground pepper

4 skinless bone-in chicken breasts (about 2 pounds)

1 pound small red potatoes, quartered

½ cup water

1. Preheat oven to 425° F.

2. Combine the lemon juice, 1 tablespoon of the oil, the garlic, oregano, marjoram, ½ teaspoon of the salt, and ⅛ teaspoon of the pepper in a large bowl. Add the chicken, tossing well to coat, and marinate 20 minutes.

3. Meanwhile, combine the remaining ½ tablespoon oil, ¼ teaspoon salt, and ⅛ teaspoon pepper in a medium bowl. Add the potatoes and toss well to coat. Place a wire rack in the center of a large roasting pan. Arrange the potatoes around the rack and roast 20 minutes.

4. Remove the chicken from the marinade; reserve marinade. Remove the potatoes from the oven, and place the chicken on the wire rack. Add the water to the reserved marinade and pour over the chicken and potatoes. Roast chicken and potatoes 20 minutes; baste with the pan juices. Return the pan to the oven and roast until an instant-read thermometer inserted in the thickest part of the chicken registers 170° F, about 15–20 minutes longer.

Per serving (1 chicken breast with ¼ of potatoes): 301 Cal, 9 g Fat, 2 g Sat Fat, 90 mg Chol, 519 mg Sod, 17 g Carb, 3 g Fib, 36 g Prot, 34 mg Calc. **POINTS: 6.**

greek diner delights

Lamb Souvlaki
with Rice

Lamb Souvlaki with Rice

MAKES 6 SERVINGS

This classic dish of marinated meat on skewers is a take-out favorite. Serve with warm pita bread and a generous dollop of garlicky Tzatziki [page 63].

1 tablespoon extra-virgin olive oil

2 cloves garlic, minced

1 teaspoon dried oregano

½ teaspoon dried thyme

1½ pounds boneless leg of lamb, trimmed of all visible fat, cut into 30 cubes

2 small red onions, root end left intact and cut into 6 wedges each

1 large green bell pepper, seeded and cut into 12 pieces

½ teaspoon salt

⅛ teaspoon freshly ground pepper

¾ cup long-grain white rice, cooked according to package directions

1. To make the marinade, combine the oil, garlic, oregano, and thyme in a large zip-close plastic bag; mix well. Add the lamb, seal the bag, and turn several times to coat. Marinate the lamb at room temperature 30 minutes or refrigerate overnight.

2. Preheat broiler. Spray a broiler pan with nonstick spray; set aside.

3. Thread 5 lamb cubes, 2 onion wedges, and 2 bell pepper pieces onto each of 6 (12-inch) metal skewers, alternating the ingredients. Transfer skewers to the broiler pan.

4. Broil the skewers 4 inches from the heat, turning at least once, until the vegetables are tender and the lamb is cooked through, 8–10 minutes. Serve with the rice.

Per serving (1 skewer with ¼ cup rice): 291 Cal, 9 g Fat, 3 g Sat Fat, 73 mg Chol, 252 mg Sod, 25 g Carb, 1 g Fib, 26 g Prot, 31 mg Calc. *POINTS: 6.*

greek diner delights

Aegean Roasted Red Snapper

MAKES 4 SERVINGS

A whole roasted fish certainly is impressive company fare, and serving it is easier than you think. The snapper is covered with garlic, herbs, and a fresh tomato sauce to ensure a moist and succulent result. Scoring the snapper with a sharp knife allows the seasonings to thoroughly penetrate the fish—and looks pretty to boot.

1½ tablespoons extra-virgin olive oil
1 onion, thinly sliced
1 celery stalk, chopped
2 cloves garlic, minced
1 teaspoon dried oregano
1 pound fresh tomatoes, chopped
½ teaspoon salt
¼ teaspoon freshly ground pepper
3½ pounds whole red snapper with head and tail, cleaned
2 tablespoons fresh lemon juice

1. Preheat oven to 500° F. Line a jelly-roll pan with foil and lightly spray with nonstick spray; set aside.

2. Heat a large nonstick skillet over medium-high heat. Swirl in 1 tablespoon oil, then add the onion, celery, garlic, and oregano. Cook until onion softens, 4–5 minutes. Add the tomatoes, ¼ teaspoon of the salt, and ⅛ teaspoon of the pepper; cook 3 minutes. Remove from the heat.

3. With a sharp knife, make 4 deep cuts (down to the bone) crosswise on each side of the fish. Rub the fish with the remaining ½ tablespoon oil. Sprinkle with the remaining ¼ teaspoon salt and ⅛ teaspoon pepper; transfer to the jelly-roll pan. Cover fish with the tomato mixture, then pour the lemon juice over the tomatoes.

4. Cover the fish loosely with foil. Roast 35–40 minutes or until fish flakes easily with a fork.

Per serving (¼ of snapper): 221 Cal, 7 g Fat, 1 g Sat Fat, 49 mg Chol, 374 mg Sod, 10 g Carb, 2 g Fib, 29 g Prot, 68 mg Calc. **POINTS: 5.**

clever cook's tip

When buying a whole fish, look for clear, bright eyes. The tail should not be curled or dried up. A fish's gills should be cherry-red; the scales should be tight and have a good sheen. Rinse the fish as soon as you get it home, before refrigerating. Then place the fish in a colander half filled with ice, pour more ice over it, and set the colander over a large bowl. Refrigerate until ready to prepare.

Phyllo Purses with Dried Fruit Compote

MAKES 6 SERVINGS

This versatile compote can work with any number of dried fruits: Try substituting dates or dried pears for the figs, sweetened dried cherries for the raisins, or dried apples for the apricots.

¼ **pound dried figs (about ½ cup), quartered**

¼ **pound dried apricots (about 1½ cups), sliced**

½ **cup packed golden raisins**

½ **cup orange juice**

½ **cup water**

⅓ **cup honey**

1 **cinnamon stick**

1 **teaspoon vanilla extract**

2 **tablespoons sliced almonds**

4 **(12 x 17-inch) sheets phyllo dough, thawed according to package directions if frozen**

1. Preheat oven to 350° F. Spray a baking sheet with nonstick spray; set aside.

2. To make the compote, combine the figs, apricots, raisins, orange juice, water, honey, cinnamon stick, and vanilla in a medium saucepan. Bring to a boil, reduce the heat to medium-low and simmer, stirring occasionally, until the fruit plumps and the liquid becomes syrupy, 12–15 minutes. Remove the compote from the heat; discard the cinnamon stick. Cool 10 minutes, then stir in the almonds.

3. Place one sheet of phyllo with the long side facing you on a work surface (cover remaining phyllo with plastic wrap to retain moisture). Lightly spray with nonstick spray; top with a second phyllo sheet and lightly spray with nonstick spray. Repeat with the remaining phyllo sheets to form a stack. With a sharp knife or pizza wheel, cut the phyllo into 6 equal squares. Place ¼ cup of the compote in the center of each square. Working one square at a time, gather the four corners of the square together to enclose the compote. Twist the gathered phyllo lightly to seal the packet and form a "purse." Transfer purse to the baking sheet; repeat with the remaining phyllo, nonstick spray, and compote to make 6 purses.

4. Spray the purses lightly with nonstick spray. Bake until crisp and golden, 12–15 minutes. Serve warm.

Per serving (1 purse): 253 Cal, 2 g Fat, 0 g Sat Fat, 0 mg Chol, 68 mg Sod, 60 g Carb, 5 g Fib, 3 g Prot, 53 mg Calc. **POINTS: 4.**

clever cook's tip

This dessert can be made in advance. Prepare as directed through Step 3, except transfer the purses to a large plate, then spray lightly with nonstick spray and cover with plastic wrap. Refrigerate overnight. Allow the purses to come to room temperature (keeping them covered with plastic wrap). Uncover purses, transfer to the baking sheet, and bake as directed.

Yogurt with Honey
and Walnuts and
Phyllo Purses
with Dried Fruit
Compote

Yogurt with Honey and Walnuts

MAKES 6 SERVINGS

Yiaourti, Greek yogurt, is distinctively thicker, creamier, and fattier than our American counterpart. Yet we mimicked the richer taste and consistency with homemade yogurt cheese.

½ **cup walnut halves**
2 **cups yogurt cheese***
6 **tablespoons honey**

1. Heat a large skillet over medium heat. Add the walnuts and toast, shaking the pan often, until the nuts are fragrant, 6–7 minutes. Transfer the nuts to a cutting board; cool and coarsely chop.

2. Spoon the yogurt cheese in each of 6 bowls. Top each serving with the honey, then sprinkle with the toasted walnuts.

*To make 2 cups yogurt cheese, spoon 1 (32-ounce) container plain nonfat yogurt into a coffee filter or a cheese-cloth–lined strainer; set over a bowl and let stand in the refrigerator 2 hours or overnight. Discard the liquid.

Per serving (⅓ cup yogurt with 1 tablespoon honey and 1 tablespoon walnuts): 203 Cal, 6 g Fat, 1 g Sat Fat, 3 mg Chol, 117 mg Sod, 30 g Carb, 1 g Fib, 10 g Prot, 311 mg Calc. *POINTS: 4.*

clever cook's tip

Use plain, not vanilla-flavored, yogurt for the most successful results.

4

viva mexico!

Corn-and-Jalapeño Quesadillas

Quesadillas are the Mexican version of the grilled cheese sandwich. One wedge makes a tasty appetizer, but two or three wedges are perfect when you're looking for a quick lunch. Canned black beans and diced zucchini or yellow squash make excellent substitutions for the corn and bell pepper filling.

---

1 teaspoon olive oil

1 cup fresh or frozen corn kernels

1 red bell pepper, seeded and diced

1 jalapeño pepper, seeded and minced (wear gloves to prevent irritation)

4 scallions, chopped

2 garlic cloves, minced

1 tablespoon chili powder

½ teaspoon ground cumin

¼ teaspoon salt

½ cup prepared salsa

8 (6-inch) fat-free flour tortillas

½ cup shredded reduced-fat cheddar cheese

---

1. Preheat the oven to 450° F. Spray a large nonstick baking sheet with nonstick spray; set aside.

2. Heat a medium nonstick skillet over medium-high heat. Swirl in the oil, then add the corn, bell pepper, jalapeño, scallions, garlic, chili powder, cumin, and salt. Cook, stirring occasionally, until the vegetables are tender, about 8 minutes. Remove from the heat and stir in the salsa.

3. Place 1 tortilla on the baking sheet. Top with one-quarter of the corn mixture and 2 tablespoons of the cheddar. Place another tortilla on top. Repeat with the remaining tortillas, corn mixture, and cheese to make 4 quesadillas.

4. Lightly spray the top of each tortilla with nonstick spray. Bake until the tortillas are golden and the cheese is melted, about 8 minutes. Transfer the quesadillas to a cutting board and cut each into 4 wedges.

Per serving (1 wedge): 84 Cal, 1 g Fat, 0 g Sat Fat, 2 mg Chol, 177 mg Sod, 16 g Carb, 1 g Fib, 3 g Prot, 74 mg Calc. *POINTS: 2.*

clever cook's tip

If using fresh corn, you will need about 2 medium ears to get 1 cup of kernels.

Chicken Empanadas

MAKES 12 SERVINGS

Empanadas, a favorite Mexican and Spanish appetizer, are sweet- or savory-filled turnovers wrapped in pastry. The crust used in this recipe is made from reduced-fat baking mix, resulting in a tender, flaky dough. The filling is a tantalizing sweet-spicy chicken mixture.

1 teaspoon olive oil
½ pound ground skinless chicken breast
1 small onion, finely chopped
½ cup seeded and finely chopped green bell pepper
2 garlic cloves, minced
¼ cup tomato sauce
⅓ cup raisins
12 small pimiento-stuffed olives, chopped
½ teaspoon ground cinnamon
½ teaspoon ground cumin
¼ teaspoon ground allspice
¼ teaspoon salt
1 cup + 2 tablespoons reduced-fat all-purpose baking mix
⅓ cup low-fat (1%) milk
1 large egg, lightly beaten with 1 tablespoon water

1. To make the filling, heat a medium nonstick skillet over medium-high heat. Swirl in the oil, then add the chicken, onion, bell pepper, and garlic. Cook, breaking up the chicken with a wooden spoon, until the chicken is browned and the vegetables are tender, about 8 minutes. Stir in the tomato sauce, raisins, olives, cinnamon, cumin, allspice, and salt. Cook over medium-low heat until the flavors are blended, about 5 minutes. Remove from the heat and set aside.

2. Preheat the oven to 400° F. Spray a large nonstick baking sheet with nonstick spray; set aside.

3. Combine the baking mix and milk in a small bowl, stirring with a fork, until a soft dough forms. Turn the dough onto a lightly floured surface. Knead the dough 10 times; cut into 12 pieces. Roll each piece of dough into a 4-inch circle.

4. Spoon about 2 tablespoons of the filling onto one-half of each circle of dough. Fold the dough over into a half-moon shape. Press the edges of the dough with the tines of a fork to seal. Place the empanadas on the baking sheet and brush lightly with the egg mixture. Bake until the tops are golden, about 12 minutes. Serve warm.

Per serving (1 empanada): 99 Cal, 3 g Fat, 1 g Sat Fat, 28 mg Chol, 312 mg Sod, 13 g Carb, 1 g Fib, 6 g Prot, 32 mg Calc. **POINTS: 2.**

clever cook's tip

To make ahead, place the unbaked empanadas in a single layer on a baking sheet. Cover them with foil and freeze until firm, about 2 hours. Then transfer them to a large zip-close plastic freezer bag and freeze for up to 2 months. To bake, transfer the frozen empanadas to a baking sheet and bake for approximately the same amount of time called for in this recipe.

viva mexico!

Hearty Black Bean and Sausage Soup

MAKES 6 SERVINGS

This soup gets its distinctive flavors from sweet Italian turkey sausage, jalapeño peppers, and sparkling fresh cilantro. Freeze any leftovers and simply reheat in the microwave. Serve alongside a leafy green salad with cherry tomatoes.

½ pound sweet Italian turkey sausage links
1 teaspoon olive oil
1 onion, finely chopped
2 garlic cloves, minced
2 jalapeño peppers, seeded and minced (wear gloves to prevent irritation)
3 (15½-ounce) cans black beans, rinsed and drained
4 cups low-sodium chicken broth
½ cup chopped fresh cilantro

1. Spray a large nonstick saucepan with nonstick spray and set over medium-low heat. Add the sausage and cook until browned on all sides and cooked through, about 15 minutes. Transfer the sausage to a plate. When the sausage is cool enough to handle, cut into ½-inch-thick slices.

2. Heat the oil over medium heat in the same saucepan, then add the onion, garlic, and jalapeños. Cook, stirring occasionally, until tender, about 8 minutes. Stir in the beans and broth; bring to a boil. Reduce the heat and simmer, covered, until the flavors are blended, about 8 minutes.

3. Transfer 2 cups of the bean mixture to a blender or food processor and puree. Stir the puree and the sausage into the soup. Simmer, uncovered, until the soup is heated through, about 5 minutes. Remove from the heat, stir in the cilantro, and serve.

Per serving (scant 1½ cups): 221 Cal, 6 g Fat, 2 g Sat Fat, 18 mg Chol, 582 mg Sod, 25 g Carb, 9 g Fib, 16 g Prot, 67 mg Calc. **POINTS: 4.**

Classic Tortilla Soup

MAKES 4 SERVINGS 🔥

Toasted tortilla strips give this soup its characteristic flavor and texture. For a protein boost (and an extra 3 **POINTS** per serving), add 2 cups of leftover turkey to the soup during the last 5 minutes of simmering.

- 1 teaspoon olive oil
- 1 onion, chopped
- 1 green bell pepper, seeded and chopped
- 2 garlic cloves, minced
- 1 tablespoon chili powder
- 2 teaspoons ground cumin
- 4 cups low-sodium chicken broth
- 1 (14½-ounce) can stewed tomatoes
- 1 tablespoon fresh lime juice
- 2 teaspoons grated lime rind
- 8 drops hot pepper sauce
- ¼ cup chopped fresh cilantro
- 2 (6-inch) corn tortillas, cut into ½-inch strips
- ¼ cup shredded Monterey Jack cheese

1. Heat a large nonstick saucepan over medium-high heat. Swirl in the oil, then add the onion, bell pepper, and garlic. Cook, stirring occasionally, until the vegetables are tender, about 8 minutes. Add the chili powder and cumin; cook 1 minute.

2. Stir in the broth and tomatoes; bring to a boil. Reduce the heat and simmer, uncovered, 25 minutes. Remove from the heat and stir in the lime juice, lime rind, hot sauce, and cilantro.

3. Meanwhile, spray a large nonstick skillet with nonstick spray and set over medium-high heat. Add the tortilla strips and cook, turning occasionally, until crisp and golden, about 5 minutes. Stir the tortilla strips and Monterey Jack into the soup. Serve at once.

Per serving (2 cups): 163 Cal, 6 g Fat, 2 g Sat Fat, 10 mg Chol, 378 mg Sod, 23 g Carb, 4 g Fib, 8 g Prot, 155 mg Calc. **POINTS: 3.**

Fajita Salad with Salsa Vinaigrette

MAKES 4 SERVINGS

There are countless ways you can enjoy this delicious, fat-free salsa vinaigrette: Use it to top baked potatoes, serve alongside an omelet, spoon over grilled meats and vegetables, or serve as is with baked tortilla chips. Make it with mild, medium, or hot salsa to suit your taste. Prepare a double batch to keep some on hand—it will stay fresh several days in the refrigerator.

½ cup prepared salsa

¼ cup chopped red onion

2 tablespoons chopped fresh cilantro

1 tablespoon fresh lime juice

1 tablespoon balsamic vinegar

1 teaspoon Dijon mustard

¼ teaspoon salt

4 (¼ pound) skinless boneless chicken breasts

1 tablespoon Cajun seasoning

1 teaspoon olive oil

4 cups mixed salad greens

1 red bell pepper, seeded and thinly sliced

1 yellow bell pepper, seeded and thinly sliced

1 tomato, chopped

½ avocado, peeled and chopped

1. To make the vinaigrette, puree the salsa, onion, cilantro, lime juice, vinegar, mustard, and salt in a food processor or blender. Transfer the vinaigrette to a bowl; set aside.

2. Sprinkle both sides of the chicken with the Cajun seasoning. Heat a medium nonstick skillet over medium-high heat. Swirl in the oil, then add the chicken and cook until lightly browned and just cooked through, about 4 minutes on each side. Transfer the chicken to a cutting board. Let stand 5 minutes, then slice into ½-inch-thick strips.

3. Place the salad greens and bell peppers in a large bowl. Top with the chicken strips, tomato, and avocado. Serve with the Salsa Vinaigrette.

Per serving (1½ cups salad with ⅓ cup vinaigrette): 234 Cal, 8 g Fat, 2 g Sat Fat, 63 mg Chol, 819 mg Sod, 15 g Carb, 5 g Fib, 26 g Prot, 73 mg Calc. *POINTS: 5.*

clever cook's tip

Be sure to let the chicken rest for 5 minutes before slicing—this helps keep it tender and juicy. If you slice it before it's had a few minutes to rest, the juices will run out, making the chicken dry.

Fajita Salad with
Salsa Vinaigrette

Mexican-Style Stuffed Potatoes

MAKES 4 SERVINGS

Perfect for lunch or a light dinner, these whipped, stuffed potatoes get their fluffy texture from using a hand mixer. Also important for that light, fluffy texture is the type of potato you use: The baking potato, such as the Idaho and russet, is low in moisture and high in starch—ideal for baking and mashing.

2 (¾-pound) baking potatoes, scrubbed
6 tablespoons nonfat sour cream
¼ cup low-fat (1%) milk
¼ teaspoon salt
8 drops hot pepper sauce
4 scallions, chopped
¼ cup shredded reduced-fat cheddar cheese
¼ cup prepared salsa
2 tablespoons chopped fresh cilantro

1. Preheat the oven to 425° F. Place the potatoes on the middle oven rack and bake until fork-tender, 45–55 minutes. Leave the oven on.

2. Cut the potatoes lengthwise in half. Scoop out the pulp into a medium bowl, leaving ½-inch border attached to the skin. Reserve the shells. With an electric mixer on medium speed, beat the potato pulp, sour cream, milk, salt, and hot sauce until smooth and creamy. Stir in the scallions.

3. Spoon the potato mixture back into the shells and sprinkle with the cheddar. Place on a small baking sheet. Bake until the filling is hot and the cheese is melted, about 10 minutes. Top with the salsa and cilantro.

Per serving (1 stuffed potato half): 205 Cal, 2 g Fat, 1 g Sat Fat, 7 mg Chol, 299 mg Sod, 41 g Carb, 4 g Fib, 7 g Prot, 132 mg Calc. **POINTS: 3.**

clever cook's tip

Avoid using a food processor to whip potatoes as it tends to overmix them, creating an unpleasant gummy texture.

Spinach, Rice, and Black Bean Burritos

MAKES 8 SERVINGS

Here's an inexpensive yet satisfying way to quickly feed a crowd of hungry teenagers.

2 cups water
1 cup long-grain white rice
½ teaspoon olive oil
1 onion, chopped
1 garlic clove, minced
½ teaspoon ground cumin
¼ teaspoon salt
2 cups spinach, cleaned and coarsely chopped
¾ cup tomato sauce
½ cup canned black beans, rinsed and drained
4 (10-inch) fat-free flour tortillas
¼ cup nonfat sour cream
¼ cup chopped fresh cilantro
¼ cup sliced pitted ripe olives

1. Bring the water to a boil in a medium saucepan. Add the rice and simmer, covered, over low heat, until the liquid is absorbed and the rice is tender, about 20 minutes. Remove from the heat and set aside.

2. Meanwhile, heat a large nonstick skillet over medium heat. Swirl in the oil, then add the onion, garlic, cumin, and salt. Cook, stirring occasionally, until the onion softens, about 8 minutes. Stir in the spinach, tomato sauce, and beans; bring to a boil. Reduce the heat and simmer, uncovered, stirring occasionally, until the spinach begins to wilt, about 3 minutes. Stir in the rice and heat through.

3. Stack the tortillas on a microwaveproof plate. Cover with plastic wrap and microwave on High 1 minute. Spoon the rice and bean mixture (about 1 cup) onto each warm tortilla. Top with the sour cream, cilantro, and olives. Fold the sides over and roll up to enclose the filling. Cut each burrito in half.

Per serving (½ burrito): 250 Cal, 1 g Fat, 0 g Sat Fat, 1 mg Chol, 453 mg Sod, 52 g Carb, 3 g Fib, 7 g Prot, 124 mg Calc. **POINTS: 4.**

clever cook's tip

To cut down on the prep and cooking times, use 3 cups cooked instant rice (brown or white) and buy fresh chopped spinach from your supermarket's salad bar.

Spicy Shrimp Kebabs with Tomatillo Salsa

MAKES 4 SERVINGS 🔥

Native to Mexico, tomatillos are little green tomatoes with a thin papery husk. They have a slightly tart lemony flavor and are used in a variety of Mexican dishes, such as chili, salsa, and guacamole.

4 scallions, finely chopped

¼ cup + 2 tablespoons chopped fresh cilantro

4 tablespoons fresh lime juice

2 garlic cloves, minced

1 tablespoon chopped chipotles en adobo

1 teaspoon olive oil

1 tablespoon dried oregano

½ teaspoon sugar

½ teaspoon salt

16 medium shrimp, peeled, deveined, and butterflied

1 yellow bell pepper, seeded and cut into 1-inch pieces

1 large red onion, cut into 8 wedges

6 medium fresh tomatillos, chopped (remove papery husk and rinse before chopping)

1 cup cherry tomatoes, halved

½ cup finely chopped red onion

1. To marinate the shrimp and vegetables, combine the scallions, ¼ cup of the cilantro, 2 tablespoons of the lime juice, garlic, chipotles, oil, oregano, sugar, and ¼ teaspoon of the salt in a large zip-close plastic bag; add the shrimp, bell pepper, and onion wedges. Squeeze out the air and seal the bag; turn to coat the shrimp and vegetables. Refrigerate, turning the bag occasionally, about 20 minutes.

2. To make the salsa, combine the tomatillos, tomatoes, chopped onion, and the remaining 2 tablespoons cilantro, 2 tablespoons lime juice, and ¼ teaspoon salt in a medium bowl; set aside.

3. Spray the grill or broiler rack with nonstick spray; prepare the grill or preheat the broiler.

4. Remove the shrimp and vegetables from the marinade; discard the marinade. Thread the shrimp, bell pepper, and onion onto 4 (12-inch) metal skewers, alternating the ingredients. Grill or broil the kebabs 5 inches from the heat until the vegetables are tender and the shrimp is just opaque in the center, about 3 minutes on each side. Serve with the salsa.

Per serving (1 skewer with ¾ cup salsa): 97 Cal, 2 g Fat, 0 g Sat Fat, 37 mg Chol, 232 mg Sod, 16 g Carb, 3 g Fib, 7 g Prot, 46 mg Calc.
POINTS: 2.

Tacos Veracruz

MAKES 6 SERVINGS

A great change from beef or chicken, these tacos are filled with chunks of cod and sweet, sautéed onions. Substitute swordfish, sea bass, tuna, or salmon for the cod, if desired. Take care not to overcook the fish, as it easily becomes tough and dry.

- 6 taco shells
- 1 teaspoon olive oil
- 1 onion, thinly sliced
- 2 garlic cloves, minced
- 1 tomato, chopped
- 1 pound cod fillet, cut into 1-inch pieces
- 1 tablespoon Cajun seasoning
- ½ cup prepared taco sauce
- 1 cup shredded lettuce
- 3 scallions, thinly sliced

1. Preheat the oven to 400° F. Place the taco shells on a baking sheet and warm them in the oven, about 8 minutes; keep warm.

2. Meanwhile, heat a large nonstick skillet over medium heat. Swirl in the oil, then add the onion and garlic. Cook, stirring occasionally, until well softened, about 8 minutes. Add the tomato and cook, stirring occasionally, until the tomato begins to soften, about 4 minutes. Transfer the onion mixture to a bowl and keep warm. Wipe the skillet clean.

3. Spray the skillet with nonstick spray and set over high heat. Add the cod and sprinkle with the seasoning. Cook, turning occasionally with tongs, until the fish is browned on the outside and just opaque in the center, about 8 minutes. Gently stir in the taco sauce and heat through. Transfer the cod mixture to the onion mixture in the bowl, tossing gently with a rubber spatula until blended.

4. Line each taco shell with the lettuce. Spoon about ⅓ cup of the cod mixture into each shell. Sprinkle each with the scallions. Serve at once.

Per serving (1 taco): 121 Cal, 4 g Fat, 1 g Sat Fat, 20 mg Chol, 410 mg Sod, 12 g Carb, 2 g Fib, 10 g Prot, 27 mg Calc. ***POINTS: 2.***

clever cook's tip

For a wrap sandwich, roll the filling in warmed flour tortillas instead of using taco shells.

Chimichurri Steak with Jicama Salsa

Chimichurri Steak with Jicama Salsa

MAKES 4 SERVINGS

Chimichurri is a tangy condiment used in many Spanish dishes. It's a perfect accompaniment to grilled meats, vegetables, and salads. Here, we mix half of the chimichurri with the vegetables to make the salsa and use the other half to drizzle over the steak.

- ½ cup chopped fresh cilantro
- ½ cup chopped fresh parsley
- 2 tablespoons red-wine vinegar
- 2 tablespoons fresh lime juice
- 1 tablespoon extra-virgin olive oil
- 2 garlic cloves, chopped
- ½ teaspoon salt
- ¼ teaspoon crushed red pepper
- 1 small jicama, peeled and cut into ½-inch cubes
- 4 medium tomatillos, chopped (remove papery husk and rinse before chopping)
- ½ avocado, peeled and cut into ½-inch chunks
- ½ red onion, finely chopped
- 1 (1-pound) boneless sirloin steak, trimmed of all visible fat

1. To make the chimichurri, puree the cilantro, parsley, vinegar, lime juice, oil, garlic, ¼ teaspoon of the salt, and the crushed red pepper in a food processor or blender. Transfer to a bowl.

2. To make the salsa, combine the jicama, tomatillos, avocado, and onion in a medium bowl. Add half of the chimichurri and toss to coat. Set aside.

3. Spray a nonstick ridged grill pan with nonstick spray and set over medium-high heat. Season the steak with the remaining ¼ teaspoon salt. Sear the steak until browned, 3–5 minutes. Turn over; cook until done to taste, 5–8 minutes longer for medium. Transfer the steak to a cutting board; let stand 5 minutes. Thinly slice the steak across the grain, then arrange on a platter. Drizzle with the remaining chimichurri and serve with the salsa.

Per serving (¼ of steak with 2 tablespoons chimichurri and ½ cup salsa): 294 Cal, 14 g Fat, 4 g Sat Fat, 75 mg Chol, 360 mg Sod, 15 g Carb, 7 g Fib, 28 g Prot, 42 mg Calc. **POINTS: 6.**

clever cook's tip

If you want to have a supply of chimichurri on hand, this recipe can easily be doubled. It can also be made ahead. Combine all the ingredients as directed except the cilantro. Cover and refrigerate up to 3 days, then add the chopped cilantro just before serving.

Healthy Beef-and-Bean Tacos

MAKES 4 SERVINGS

A traditional and satisfying Mexican favorite, beef tacos are made here with fat-free refried beans, which are a delicious and good-for-you meat extender. These beans are also terrific used as a thickener in soups, as a base for your favorite sandwich wraps, or as a tasty dip for raw veggies.

1 teaspoon olive oil
½ pound lean ground beef (10% or less fat)
1 onion, finely chopped
2 garlic cloves, minced
3 tablespoons taco seasoning mix
½ cup water
1¼ cups fat-free refried beans
8 taco shells
1 cup shredded lettuce
1 large tomato, diced
2 tablespoons sliced pitted ripe olives
½ cup finely chopped red onion
½ cup nonfat sour cream

1. Preheat the oven to 400° F. Place the taco shells on a baking sheet and warm them in the oven, about 8 minutes; keep warm.

2. Meanwhile, heat a large nonstick skillet over medium-high heat. Swirl in the oil, then add the beef, onion, garlic, and seasoning mix. Cook, breaking up the beef with a wooden spoon, until browned, about 8 minutes. Stir in the water. Cook, until the liquid has evaporated, about 3 minutes. Stir in the beans and heat through.

3. Spoon about ¼ cup of the beef mixture into each taco. Top each with the lettuce, tomato, olives, onion, and sour cream.

Per serving (2 tacos): 318 Cal, 9 g Fat, 1 g Sat Fat, 25 mg Chol, 1,123 mg Sod, 41 g Carb, 7 g Fib, 17 g Prot, 106 mg Calc. *POINTS: 6.*

Shredded-Pork-and-Vegetable Tostadas

MAKES 4 SERVINGS

These tostadas—open-face tacos—can be whipped up in minutes. Save even more time by using leftover chopped cooked pork or chicken, instead of the pork tenderloin strips, and omit Step 1. Then simply heat the leftover meat with the cooked vegetables.

viva mexico!

1 teaspoon olive oil
½ pound pork tenderloin, trimmed of all visible fat, cut into ¼-inch-thick strips
½ teaspoon salt
1 onion, thinly sliced
1 red bell pepper, seeded and thinly sliced
1 garlic clove, minced
4 (6-inch) corn tortillas
½ cup fat-free refried beans, heated
1 tomato, chopped
¼ cup reduced-fat goat cheese, crumbled
2 tablespoons chopped fresh cilantro

1. Heat a medium nonstick skillet over medium–high heat. Swirl in the oil, then add the pork and sprinkle with the salt. Cook, tossing the pork occasionally, until browned, about 6 minutes; transfer to a plate.

2. Add the onion, bell pepper, and garlic to the skillet. Cook, stirring occasionally, until the vegetables are tender, about 8 minutes. Return the pork to the skillet and cook until heated through, about 2 minutes. Remove from the heat.

3. Meanwhile, heat a small nonstick skillet over medium–high heat. Add 1 tortilla and cook over medium heat until crisp, about 3 minutes on each side. Transfer the tortilla to a plate. Repeat with the remaining tortillas.

4. Spread the beans over the tortillas, then top with the pork mixture, tomato, goat cheese, and cilantro.

Per serving (1 tostada): 199 Cal, 5 g Fat, 2 g Sat Fat, 35 mg Chol, 514 mg Sod, 23 g Carb, 4 g Fib, 16 g Prot, 71 mg Calc. *POINTS: 4.*

Pork Kebabs with Mango Salsa

MAKES 4 SERVINGS

Ripe juicy mangos and creamy black beans spiked with red onion, cilantro, jalapeño, and lime juice make a perfect and satisfying accompaniment to broiled pork. Since metal-skewer handles can become extremely hot, use tongs or hot pads to transfer the kebabs to plates.

1 (15-ounce) can black beans, rinsed and drained
1 mango, peeled, pitted, and cut into ½-inch cubes
1 red bell pepper, finely diced
½ red onion, chopped
3 tablespoons chopped cilantro
1 jalapeño pepper, seeded and minced (wear gloves to prevent irritation)
2 tablespoons fresh lime juice
1 tablespoon honey
2 teaspoons Dijon mustard
⅛ teaspoon salt
¾ pound pork tenderloin, trimmed of all visible fat, cut into 1-inch chunks
2 tablespoons white-wine vinegar
1 tablespoon dried oregano
2 teaspoons chili powder
½ teaspoon cumin
½ teaspoon olive oil

1. To make the salsa, combine the beans, mango, bell pepper, onion, cilantro, and jalapeño in a medium bowl. Whisk together the lime juice, honey, mustard, and salt in a small bowl. Pour the dressing over the bean mixture; toss to coat. Cover and refrigerate until ready to serve.

2. Spray the broiler rack with nonstick spray. Preheat the broiler.

3. Toss the pork, vinegar, oregano, chili powder, cumin, and oil in a medium bowl until well coated. Thread the pork onto 4 (8-inch) metal skewers. Broil 4 inches from the heat, turning often, until the meat is tender and cooked through, about 8 minutes. Serve the kebabs with the salsa.

Per serving (1 skewer with ¾ cup salsa): 263 Cal, 6 g Fat, 1 g Sat Fat, 50 mg Chol, 400 mg Sod, 32 g Carb, 7 g Fib, 23 g Prot, 83 mg Calc. *POINTS: 5.*

clever cook's tip

For best flavor, be sure to use a ripe mango. To ripen a mango, set it on the counter or in a fruit bowl for a day or two until it is slightly soft to the touch. To cut a mango, use a sharp knife to cut the fruit vertically, sliding the knife along the seed on one side. Repeat on the other side, which will give you 2 large pieces. With the tip of your knife, score the flesh in a crosshatch pattern, cutting just to, but not through, the skin. Hold the mango half with both hands and push so the mango turns inside out. Slice the cubes away from the skin.

the perfect pantry

Stock up on these south-of-the-border items and add pizzazz to your pantry.

- **Avocado:** Rich, buttery-textured fruit with mild, gentle nutty flavor; most common varieties: the thin, smooth green-skinned Fuerte and the black, pebbly-skinned Haas, which is more often used in Mexican dishes.
- **Black beans:** Black-skinned beans with cream-colored flesh, commonly used in Mexican cooking; sweet flavor.
- **Chili powder:** Seasoning that usually includes dried chiles, garlic, oregano, cumin, coriander, and cloves; heat can range from mild to fiery, depending on the brand used.
- **Chipotles en adobo:** Dried, smoked jalapeño peppers that are pickled and canned in adobo sauce; smoky-sweet flavor.
- **Cilantro:** Bright green leaves and stems of the coriander plant; zesty, pungent taste and fragrance.
- **Cumin:** Aromatic, nutty-flavored spice used alone or to make chili powder.
- **Enchilada sauce:** Rich red or green chile-flavored sauce used for enchiladas, meats, stews, and rice dishes.
- **Jalapeño pepper:** Small, smooth, dark green chile; flavor ranges from hot to very hot.
- **Jicama:** Large, round root vegetable with thin brown skin and white crunchy flesh; sweet, nutty flavor; used often in salsas and salads.
- **Poblano chile:** Richly flavored, dark green chile; heat can range from mild to moderately hot.
- **Refried beans:** Pinto beans that are soaked, boiled, and mashed to a thick consistency to bring out their best flavor.
- **Salsa:** Mexican word for sauce; can be cooked or uncooked; spiciness ranges from mild to fiery hot.
- **Taco sauce:** A smooth blend of tomatoes, chiles, garlic, and spices.
- **Tomatillos:** Small green tomato with a thin papery husk; lemony, herbal flavor with hint of apple; available fresh or canned.
- **Tortillas:** Round, flat, unleavened bread that resembles a very thin pancake; corn tortillas are made from corn flour (masa), flour tortillas from wheat flour.

viva mexico!

Pork Tortillas Adobo

MAKES 4 SERVINGS

Sweet, sour, and spicy meld together in these tasty tortillas. The flavors are reminiscent of years gone by in Mexico, when meats were pickled in a paste made of chiles, vinegar, and spices to help preserve them.

1 teaspoon olive oil
2 onions, sliced
½ teaspoon granulated sugar
½ teaspoon salt
¼ cup water
½ cup tomato sauce
1 tablespoon packed light brown sugar
1 teaspoon chili powder
1 teaspoon dried oregano
¼ teaspoon ground cumin
1 teaspoon cider vinegar
1 (1-pound) pork tenderloin, trimmed of all visible fat
4 (8-inch) fat-free flour tortillas

1. Heat a large nonstick skillet over medium-low heat. Swirl in the oil, then add the onions, granulated sugar, ¼ teaspoon of the salt, and the water. Cook, uncovered, stirring occasionally, until softened and lightly browned, about 20 minutes. Stir in the tomato sauce and simmer, uncovered, until the flavors are blended, 5 minutes. Remove from the heat and keep warm.

2. Preheat the oven to 450° F. Spray the rack of a roasting pan with nonstick spray and place in the pan.

3. Combine the brown sugar, chili powder, oregano, cumin, vinegar, and the remaining ¼ teaspoon salt in a small bowl. Rub the mixture all over the pork. Place the pork on the roasting rack and roast until an instant-read thermometer inserted into the thickest part of the pork registers 160° F, about 25 minutes. Transfer the pork to a carving board and let stand 10 minutes.

4. Meanwhile, wrap the tortillas in foil and place in the oven to warm for 10 minutes. Thinly slice the pork and stir into the onion mixture. Spoon about ½ cup pork mixture onto each tortilla and fold in half.

Per serving (1 tortilla): 309 Cal, 6 g Fat, 2 g Sat Fat, 67 mg Chol, 688 mg Sod, 36 g Carb, 3 g Fib, 28 g Prot, 113 mg Calc. **POINTS: 6.**

Chipotle Chicken and Rice

MAKES 6 SERVINGS

Chipotle chiles are often used to add intriguing flavor to Mexican stews, sauces, vegetable, and egg dishes. Just one chipotle adds depth of flavor, heat, and a touch of smokiness to this chicken and rice dish. You can find canned (about 7-ounce) chipotles en adobo in specialty stores or in the ethnic section of most supermarkets.

1 teaspoon olive oil
1 pound skinless boneless chicken thighs, trimmed of all visible fat, cut into 2-inch chunks
1 onion, chopped
1 green bell pepper, seeded and chopped
2 garlic cloves, minced
1 cup long-grain white rice
1 chipotle en adobo, chopped
1 can (8-ounce) tomato sauce
1 cup water
12 pimiento-stuffed olives, chopped
1 cup frozen peas

1. Heat a large nonstick skillet over medium–high heat. Swirl in the oil, then add the chicken and cook, turning occasionally, until browned, about 8 minutes. Transfer the chicken to a plate.

2. Add the onion, bell pepper, and garlic to the skillet. Cook over medium heat, stirring occasionally, until softened, about 8 minutes. Add the rice and chipotle; cook 1 minute. Stir in the chicken, tomato sauce, water, and olives; bring to a boil. Reduce the heat and simmer, covered, until the chicken is cooked through and the rice is tender, about 20 minutes. Stir in the peas and heat through.

Per serving (1 cup): 306 Cal, 8 g Fat, 2 g Sat Fat, 54 mg Chol, 615 mg Sod, 37 g Carb, 3 g Fib, 20 g Prot, 41 mg Calc. ***POINTS: 6.***

clever cook's tip

Canned chipotles en adobo can be refrigerated in an airtight container up to 1 month.

Red Roasted Chicken

MAKES 6 SERVINGS

Tinged with red from paprika, flavored with garlic and herbs, and sweetened with a touch of brown sugar, this whole roasted chicken is delicious and succulent. The seasonings are rubbed under the skin, transferring all the flavor to the meat instead of the skin, which is discarded after cooking.

1 tablespoon packed light brown sugar
1 tablespoon paprika
1 tablespoon red-wine vinegar
2 teaspoons dried oregano
1 garlic clove, mashed to a paste
½ teaspoon ground cumin
½ teaspoon salt
1 (3½-pound) roasting chicken
1 onion, quartered

1. Preheat the oven to 400° F. Spray the rack of a roasting pan with nonstick spray and place in the pan; set aside.

2. Combine the sugar, paprika, vinegar, oregano, garlic, cumin, and salt in a small bowl to make a paste.

3. Gently loosen the skin from the breast and leg portions of the chicken; rub the paste evenly under the skin. Place the onion into the cavity of the chicken. Truss the chicken and place, breast-side up, in the roasting pan.

4. Roast until an instant-read thermometer inserted in the inner thigh registers 180° F, about 1 hour and 15 minutes. Remove from the oven and let stand 10 minutes. Remove and discard the onion and skin, then carve.

Per serving (⅙ of chicken): 201 Cal, 8 g Fat, 2 g Sat Fat, 84 mg Chol, 280 mg Sod, 3 g Carb, 1 g Fib, 28 g Prot, 28 mg Calc. *POINTS: 4.*

clever cook's tip

Trussing the chicken gives it a neat appearance and helps keep the juices inside. Here's how to do it: Simply tuck the wings behind the back and tie the legs with kitchen twine. Mashing garlic into a paste is easy: Cut the cloves in half, sprinkle them with a little salt, and mash to a pulp with the tip of your knife.

Red Roasted Chicken

Chili Con Carne

MAKES 6 SERVINGS

Zesty prepared salsa and Cajun seasoning makes this chili a blue-ribbon winner. Top the chili with minced red onion and, for an extra ½ **POINT** per serving, sprinkle with 1 tablespoon of shredded reduced-fat cheddar cheese. Serve any leftovers spooned onto hamburger buns for a chili-style sloppy joe.

1 teaspoon olive oil
1 large onion, chopped
3 garlic cloves, chopped
1 (4½-ounce) can chopped mild green chiles
2 tablespoons Cajun seasoning
1 pound ground skinless chicken breast
1 (28-ounce) can Italian peeled tomatoes, chopped
1 cup prepared salsa
½ cup water
¼ cup chili powder
1 teaspoon sugar
½ teaspoon salt
2 (15-ounce) cans red kidney beans, rinsed and drained

1. Heat a large nonstick saucepan over medium heat. Swirl in the oil, then add the onion. Cook, stirring occasionally, until softened, about 6 minutes. Stir in the garlic, chiles, and seasoning. Cook until fragrant, about 1 minute. Add the chicken and cook, breaking up the chicken with a wooden spoon, until browned, about 8 minutes.

2. Add the tomatoes with their liquid, salsa, water, chili powder, sugar, and salt; bring to a boil. Reduce the heat and simmer, covered, until the flavors are blended and the chili thickens slightly, about 1 hour. Stir in the beans and cook until heated through.

Per serving (1⅓ cups): 247 Cal, 4 g Fat, 1 g Sat Fat, 42 mg Chol, 1,465 mg Sod, 31 g Carb, 11 g Fib, 23 g Prot, 116 mg Calc. **POINTS: 4.**

clever cook's tip

An easy way to chop canned tomatoes is to do it right in the can, using kitchen scissors.

Family-Style Chicken Enchiladas

MAKES 4 SERVINGS

Enchiladas, filled and rolled tortillas that are baked in a sauce, are a comfort-food favorite. They are also a cook's favorite because you can prepare them, then relax a little while they bake. They can be made with corn or flour tortillas. Adobo seasoning is an all-purpose seasoning used to enhance many Mexican dishes. It can be found in the spice section of your supermarket.

1 teaspoon olive oil
3 (¼ pound) skinless boneless chicken breasts, cut into ½-inch-thick strips
2 onions, sliced
2 garlic cloves, minced
½ teaspoon adobo seasoning
1 (19-ounce) can enchilada sauce
4 (8-inch) fat-free flour tortillas
½ cup shredded reduced-fat cheddar cheese
4 small ripe olives, sliced

1. Preheat the oven to 375° F. Spray a 7 x 11-inch baking dish with nonstick spray; set aside.

2. Heat a large nonstick skillet over medium-high heat. Swirl in the oil, then add the chicken. Cook, turning occasionally, until browned, about 8 minutes. Transfer the chicken to a plate.

3. Add the onions, garlic, and seasoning to the skillet. Cook over medium heat, stirring occasionally, until the onions are tender, about 8 minutes. Stir in the chicken and ½ cup of the enchilada sauce; heat through.

4. Meanwhile, wrap the tortillas in foil and place in the oven to warm for 10 minutes.

5. Fill each tortilla with one-fourth of the chicken mixture. Roll up and place, seam-side down, in the baking dish. Spoon the remaining enchilada sauce over the top. Sprinkle with the cheddar and olives. Cover with foil and bake 15 minutes. Uncover and bake until the edges of the enchiladas just begin to brown and the cheese is melted and bubbly, about 10 minutes longer. Let stand 5 minutes before serving.

Per serving (1 enchilada): 342 Cal, 9 g Fat, 2 g Sat Fat, 55 mg Chol, 738 mg Sod, 40 g Carb, 2 g Fib, 25 g Prot, 207 mg Calc. *POINTS: 7.*

viva mexico!

Skinny Chimichangas

MAKES 4 SERVINGS

Traditionally, chimichangas are meaty deep-fried burritos. Our trimmer version uses ground turkey in the filling and the chimichangas are baked, instead of deep-fried. The result is a crispy burrito with a moist, flavorful filling.

½ pound ground skinless turkey breast

1 onion, finely chopped

1 garlic clove, minced

2 teaspoons chili powder

1 teaspoon dried oregano

½ teaspoon ground cumin

1 (8-ounce) can tomato sauce

2 tablespoons chopped mild green chiles

⅓ cup shredded reduced-fat cheddar cheese

4 (8-inch) fat-free flour tortillas

1. Preheat the oven to 400° F. Spray a nonstick baking sheet with nonstick spray; set aside.

2. Spray a medium nonstick skillet with nonstick spray; set over medium-high heat. Add the turkey, onion, garlic, chili powder, oregano, and cumin. Cook, breaking up the turkey with a wooden spoon until browned, about 6 minutes. Stir in the tomato sauce and the chiles; bring to a boil. Reduce the heat and simmer, uncovered, until the flavors are blended and the mixture thickens slightly, about 5 minutes. Remove from the heat and stir in the cheddar.

3. Meanwhile, wrap the tortillas in foil and place in the oven to warm for 10 minutes.

4. Spoon about ½ cup of the filling into the center of each tortilla. Fold in the sides, then roll to enclose the filling. Place the chimichangas, seam-side down, on the baking sheet. Lightly spray the tops of the tortillas with nonstick spray. Bake until golden and crisp, about 20 minutes. Do not turn.

Per serving (1 chimichanga): 241 Cal, 2 g Fat, 1 g Sat Fat, 46 mg Chol, 613 mg Sod, 34 g Carb, 3 g Fib, 22 g Prot, 184 mg Calc. *POINTS: 4.*

clever cook's tip

You can top these chimichangas with your favorite salsa and, for an extra 1 *POINT* per serving, 2 tablespoons fat-free sour cream.

Easy Mexican Pizzas

MAKES 4 SERVINGS

Corn tortillas are used as the base for these tasty pizzas. Cut them into triangles for a terrific party appetizer or serve them whole for lunch or dinner. A nice variation is to substitute sweet Italian turkey sausage for the ground turkey.

1 teaspoon olive oil
½ pound ground skinless turkey breast
1 onion, chopped
3 tablespoons taco seasoning mix
1 (14½-ounce) can stewed tomatoes
¼ cup water
4 (6-inch) corn tortillas
¼ cup shredded reduced-fat cheddar cheese
8 small pitted ripe olives, chopped
1 tablespoon sliced pickled jalapeños, coarsely chopped

1. Preheat the oven to 425° F. Spray a nonstick baking sheet with nonstick spray; set aside.

2. Heat a large nonstick skillet over medium-high heat. Swirl in the oil, then add the turkey, onion, and seasoning mix. Cook, breaking up the turkey with a wooden spoon, until browned, about 7 minutes. Stir in the tomatoes and water; bring to a boil. Simmer, uncovered, over medium-high heat, until most of the liquid has evaporated, about 8 minutes.

3. Meanwhile, spray another large nonstick skillet with nonstick spray and set over medium-high heat. Add one tortilla and cook, turning occasionally, until crisp and golden, about 5 minutes. Repeat with the remaining tortillas.

4. Arrange the tortillas on the baking sheet. Spoon the turkey mixture onto the tortillas. Sprinkle each with the cheddar, olives, and jalapeños.

5. Bake until the filling is hot and the cheese is melted and bubbly, about 15 minutes.

Per serving (1 pizza): 228 Cal, 4 g Fat, 1 g Sat Fat, 45 mg Chol, 1,042 mg Sod, 28 g Carb, 4 g Fib, 20 g Prot, 150 mg Calc. *POINTS: 4.*

clever cook's tip

Pickled jalapeños add a kick to countless Mexican recipes. You can find them in jars, either sliced or whole. Once opened, store them in the refrigerator. If you own a pizza stone, increase the oven temperature to 450° F and preheat the stone for 30 minutes. Omit Step 3 and place the tortillas on the stone. Add the toppings and bake for 15 minutes.

Nachos Supreme

Nachos Supreme

MAKES 6 SERVINGS

Be as creative as you like with this recipe. Go vegetarian by eliminating the meat, increasing the black beans, and adding some corn, or up the nutrient quota by liberally sprinkling on chopped cooked spinach.

1 teaspoon olive oil

1 onion, finely chopped

1 garlic clove, minced

½ pound ground skinless turkey breast

2 tablespoons taco seasoning mix

1 (15½-ounce) can black beans, rinsed and drained

½ (8-ounce) jar taco sauce

6 (6-inch) corn tortillas, cut into quarters

½ cup shredded reduced-fat cheddar cheese

1 tablespoon sliced pickled jalapeños, chopped

1 tomato, diced

2 scallions, chopped

2 tablespoons chopped fresh cilantro

1. Heat a large nonstick skillet over medium-high heat. Swirl in the oil, then add the onion and garlic. Cook, stirring occasionally, until softened, 3–5 minutes. Add the turkey and the seasoning mix. Cook, breaking up the turkey with a wooden spoon, until browned, about 6 minutes. Stir in the beans and taco sauce. Cook, stirring occasionally, until the flavors are blended, about 5 minutes. Remove from the heat and set aside.

2. Preheat the broiler. Arrange the tortilla pieces in one layer on the broiler rack; spray the tortillas lightly with nonstick spray. Broil 4 inches from the heat, turning frequently, until crisp and golden, about 4 minutes.

3. Transfer the tortilla chips to a 9 x 13-inch broiler proof baking pan. Spoon the turkey mixture evenly over the chips. Sprinkle with the cheddar and jalapeños. Broil 4 inches from the heat until the filling is hot and the cheese is melted, about 2 minutes. Top with the tomato, scallions, and cilantro. Serve at once.

Per serving (⅙ of nachos): 215 Cal, 4 g Fat, 1 g Sat Fat, 32 mg Chol, 620 mg Sod, 28 g Carb, 5 g Fib, 18 g Prot, 148 mg Calc. **POINTS: 4.**

clever cook's tip

If you tend to cook Mexican frequently, you might find it convenient to buy taco seasoning mix in a 6- to 7-ounce container. Otherwise, it's available in individual packets.

Turkey Enchilada Casserole

MAKES 8 SERVINGS

Here's a different take on the classic enchilada: The tortillas are halved and layered with sauce and cheese, like a lasagna. The dish can be assembled and refrigerated, unbaked, the night before. Let the casserole stand at room temperature for 30 minutes, then bake according to directions. If you don't have time to let it stand, pop the casserole in the oven while it's preheating and add an extra few minutes cooking time, if necessary.

2 teaspoons olive oil
1 pound ground skinless turkey breast
1 large onion, chopped
2 garlic cloves, minced
½ teaspoon salt
1 teaspoon dried oregano
¼ teaspoon ground cumin
2 (10-ounce) cans enchilada sauce
1 (4½-ounce) can chopped mild green chiles
1 teaspoon red-wine vinegar
¼ cup chopped fresh cilantro
8 (6-inch) corn tortillas, halved
1 cup shredded reduced-fat cheddar cheese

1. Preheat the oven to 375° F. Spray a 7 x 11-inch baking dish with nonstick spray; set aside.

2. Heat a large nonstick skillet over medium-high heat. Swirl in 1 teaspoon of the oil, then add the turkey, half of the onions, half of the garlic, and ¼ teaspoon of the salt. Cook, breaking up the turkey with a wooden spoon until browned, about 8 minutes.

3. Meanwhile, heat a medium nonstick saucepan over medium heat. Swirl in the remaining 1 teaspoon oil, then add the remaining onions, garlic, ¼ teaspoon salt, the oregano, and cumin. Cook, stirring occasionally, until well softened, about 8 minutes. Stir in the enchilada sauce, chiles, and vinegar; bring to a boil. Reduce the heat and simmer, covered, until the flavors are blended, about 10 minutes. Remove from the heat and stir in the cilantro.

4. Arrange one-third of the tortilla halves in an overlapping layer on the bottom of the dish. Spoon one-third of the turkey mixture over the top; top with one-third of the sauce and sprinkle with one-third of the cheddar. Repeat the layering twice. Cover the pan loosely with foil and bake 20 minutes. Remove the foil and bake 5 minutes longer or until the cheese is bubbly. Let stand 10 minutes before serving.

Per serving (⅛ of casserole): 218 Cal, 6 g Fat, 2 g Sat Fat, 49 mg Chol, 588 mg Sod, 20 g Carb, 2 g Fib, 21 g Prot, 168 mg Calc. **POINTS: 4.**

Turkey Taco Salad

MAKES 4 SERVINGS

Easy to prepare and fun to eat, this nacho-style dish is a real family pleaser. Baking your own tortilla chips is so simple—and tasty—you'll never settle for store-bought again. To give the chips a little heat, sprinkle them lightly with chili powder before baking. If you're pressed for time, use store-bought fat-free tortilla chips. For an extra 1 **POINT,** top each serving with 2 tablespoons fat-free sour cream.

3 (6-inch) corn tortillas, each cut into 8 triangles
1 teaspoon olive oil
1 onion, chopped
2 garlic cloves, minced
¾ pound ground skinless turkey breast
3 tablespoons taco seasoning mix
¼ cup water
½ cup canned black beans, rinsed and drained
½ cup frozen corn kernels, thawed
¼ cup chopped fresh cilantro
3 cups torn spinach
1 tomato, chopped
¼ cup chopped scallions
¼ cup sliced ripe olives

1. Preheat the oven to 400° F. Spray a large nonstick baking sheet with nonstick spray. Arrange the tortillas, in one layer, on the baking sheet. Bake, turning occasionally, until the tortillas are crisp and the edges begin to curl slightly, about 10 minutes. Cool completely on the baking sheet on a rack.

2. Meanwhile, heat a large nonstick skillet over medium heat. Swirl in the oil, then add the onion and garlic. Cook, stirring occasionally, until golden, 7–10 minutes. Add the turkey and seasoning mix. Cook, breaking up the turkey with a wooden spoon until browned, about 8 minutes. Stir in the water and cook over medium-high heat, stirring occasionally, until the water has evaporated, about 3 minutes longer. Stir in the beans, corn, and cilantro; heat through. Remove from the heat and set aside.

3. Line a large platter with the spinach. Top with the turkey mixture, the tomato, scallions, and olives. Tuck the tortilla chips into the turkey mixture and serve at once.

Per serving (6 tortilla chips with ¾ cup turkey mixture): 262 Cal, 4 g Fat, 1 g Sat Fat, 61 mg Chol, 847 mg Sod, 31 g Carb, 6 g Fib, 27 g Prot, 102 mg Calc. **POINTS: 5.**

Sausage-Stuffed Poblanos

MAKES 4 SERVINGS

Heart-shaped dark green poblano chiles are widely used in Mexican cooking. Their heat level ranges from mild to medium. They have a rich, earthy flavor, which intensifies when they are roasted. Find them in specialty markets and in most large supermarkets.

1⅓ cups water
½ cup long-grain white rice
4 poblano chiles (about 1 pound)
1 teaspoon olive oil
1 onion, chopped
2 garlic cloves, minced
½ pound sweet Italian turkey sausage, casings removed
15 small pimiento-stuffed olives, chopped
½ teaspoon ground cumin
¼ teaspoon ground cinnamon
2 cups tomato sauce
¼ cup shredded Monterey Jack cheese

1. Bring the water to a boil in a medium saucepan. Add the rice and simmer, covered, over low heat, until the liquid is absorbed and the rice is tender, about 20 minutes. Remove from the heat and set aside.

2. Preheat the broiler. Line a baking sheet with foil; place the chiles on the baking sheet. Broil 5 inches from the heat, turning frequently with tongs, until lightly charred, about 10 minutes. Wrap the chiles in the foil and let steam for 10 minutes. When cool enough to handle, peel and cut off the tops. Gently scoop out and discard the seeds. Set the chiles aside.

3. Preheat the oven to 375° F. Spray a 7 x 11-inch baking dish with nonstick spray; set aside.

4. Meanwhile, heat a large nonstick skillet over medium heat. Swirl in the oil, then add the onion and garlic. Cook, stirring occasionally, until golden, 7–10 minutes. Add the sausage and cook, breaking up the sausage with a wooden spoon until browned, about 10 minutes. Stir in the olives, cumin, and cinnamon; cook 1 minute, then remove from the heat. Stir in the rice until blended.

5. Spoon about ½ cup filling into each of the chiles. Place the chiles in the baking dish. Top with the tomato sauce and sprinkle with the Monterey Jack. Cover loosely with foil and bake 20 minutes. Remove the foil and bake until lightly browned, 10 minutes longer.

Per serving (1 stuffed chile with ½ cup sauce): 304 Cal, 10 g Fat, 3 g Sat Fat, 29 mg Chol, 1,432 mg Sod, 42 g Carb, 4 g Fib, 15 g Prot, 114 mg Calc.
POINTS: 6.

Mexican Hot Chocolate

MAKES 6 SERVINGS

Mexican Hot Chocolate is best made using Mexican chocolate, which is sold in Hispanic markets and some large supermarkets. Mexican chocolate is a heady mix of chocolate, cinnamon, sugar, and almonds that is pressed into disks. It has a grainy texture, due to the sugar and nuts. Here, we've made our own hot chocolate recipe using a homemade mix, which you can keep on hand to make outstanding hot chocolate all winter long.

MEXICAN CHOCOLATE MIX
- 8 (1-ounce) squares semisweet chocolate, coarsely chopped
- ¼ cup sliced almonds, coarsely chopped
- ¼ cup sugar
- 1 tablespoon ground cinnamon

HOT CHOCOLATE
- 3 cups low-fat (1%) milk
- ¼ cup Mexican Chocolate Mix
- ¼ teaspoon vanilla extract
- 6 tablespoons light nondairy whipped topping
- Ground cinnamon, for sprinkling

1. To prepare the chocolate mix, process the chocolate, almonds, sugar, and cinnamon in a food processor until fine crumbs form. Transfer to an airtight container.

2. To prepare the hot chocolate, combine the milk and the chocolate mix in a medium saucepan. Bring to a simmer, stirring constantly, until the chocolate dissolves, about 5 minutes. Remove from the heat; stir in the vanilla. Pour into 6 mugs, spoon on the topping, and sprinkle with cinnamon.

Per serving (½ cup with 1 tablespoon whipped topping): 91 Cal, 4 g Fat, 2 g Sat Fat, 5 mg Chol, 62 mg Sod, 10 g Carb, 0 g Fib, 5 g Prot, 156 mg Calc. **POINTS: 2.**

clever cook's tip

This recipe makes 2 cups Mexican Chocolate Mix. You can store it in the refrigerator up to 2 weeks or freeze it up to 3 months.

5 beyond sushi

Shrimp Dumplings with Sesame Dipping Sauce

MAKES 12 SERVINGS

Wonton wrappers are surprisingly multicultural: Not only used in Asian cooking, they are also great for making ravioli and tortellini. Look for them in the refrigerator case or produce section of the supermarket. Buy only fresh-packaged wontons; when frozen wontons are thawed, the wrappers become difficult to separate and tear easily.

DIPPING SAUCE

- ¼ **cup reduced-sodium soy sauce**
- ¼ **cup seasoned rice vinegar**
- 1 **scallion, finely chopped (about 1 tablespoon)**
- 1 **teaspoon toasted sesame seeds**
- **Pinch crushed red pepper**

DUMPLINGS

- ½ **pound medium shrimp, peeled and deveined**
- 4 **scallions, coarsely chopped**
- 2 **tablespoons water chestnuts, chopped**
- 1 **tablespoon minced peeled fresh ginger**
- 1 **tablespoon dry sherry**
- 1 **tablespoon oyster sauce**
- 1 **teaspoon Asian (dark) sesame oil**
- 1 **clove garlic, minced**
- 1 **egg white**
- 36 **(3-inch) round wonton wrappers**

1. To make the dipping sauce, whisk the soy sauce, vinegar, scallions, sesame seeds, and crushed red pepper in a bowl until blended; set aside.

2. To make the filling, process the shrimp, scallions, water chestnuts, ginger, sherry, oyster sauce, sesame oil, egg white, and garlic in a food processor until smooth. Transfer to a bowl.

3. Arrange the wonton wrappers on a work surface. Place 1 teaspoon of the filling in the center of each wrapper. Brush the edges of each wonton wrapper with water, then fold into half circles, pressing the edges to seal. Repeat with the remaining filling and wrappers, to make 36 dumplings. Place completed dumplings on a baking sheet lightly covered with cornstarch and cover with damp paper towels.

4. Put 8–10 dumplings in a steamer basket; set in a saucepan over 1 inch of boiling water. Cover tightly and steam until the dumplings are cooked through, about 7 minutes. Transfer the dumplings to a serving tray. Serve immediately with the dipping sauce.

Per serving (3 dumplings with 2 teaspoons dipping sauce): 99 Cal, 1 g Fat, 0 g Sat Fat, 25 mg Chol, 479 mg Sod, 16 g Carb, 1 g Fib, 6 g Prot, 20 mg Calc. **POINTS: 2.**

clever cook's tip

To toast the sesame seeds, place them in a small dry skillet over medium-low heat. Cook, shaking the pan and stirring constantly, until fragrant, 1–2 minutes. Just watch them carefully as the seeds can burn quickly. Transfer the toasted seeds immediately to a plate to cool.

California Vegetable Rolls

MAKES 4 SERVINGS

These tasty little rolls, filled with cucumber, avocado, shredded carrot, and seasoned rice, are an excellent choice for a vegetarian buffet. The rolls are wrapped with nori, paper-thin sheets of dried seaweed, which is rich in protein, calcium, and iron. You will need a bamboo rolling mat, which is easily found in specialty kitchenware stores or Asian markets, to make the rolls. Serve the rolls with pickled ginger and reduced-sodium soy sauce for dipping, if you like.

- 3 **tablespoons seasoned rice vinegar**
- 3 **tablespoons sugar**
- ⅛ **teaspoon salt**
- 1⅓ **cups sushi or short-grain white rice**
- 1 **tablespoon wasabi (Japanese horseradish) powder**
- 4 **(8 x 7-inch) sheets nori**
- ½ **cucumber, peeled and cut into thin strips (about 1 cup)**
- 1 **avocado, peeled, pitted, and cut into strips**
- 1 **carrot, shredded (about ½ cup)**

1. Heat the vinegar, sugar, and salt in a small saucepan over medium-low heat until the sugar is dissolved, about 3 minutes. Remove from the heat; set aside and cool.

2. Place the rice in a bowl. Add enough water to cover by several inches and gently swish the grains in the bowl with your fingertips until the water becomes cloudy; drain. Repeat three or four times, until the water is clear. Drain. Combine the rice and 1½ cups fresh water in a medium saucepan; let stand 20 minutes.

3. Bring the rice mixture a boil. Cover, reduce heat to low, and simmer 15 minutes. Remove from the heat, and let the rice sit undisturbed 10 minutes. Transfer the rice to a large bowl; cool. Stir in the vinegar mixture until blended. Cover the rice with a clean, damp kitchen towel; set aside.

4. Whisk the wasabi and 1 tablespoon warm water to make a paste. Set aside. Cut nori lengthwise into eight 4 x 7-inch sheets. Place one sheet, shiny-side down with one long side side facing you, on a bamboo rolling mat. Dampen hands with water and spread ½ cup of the rice on the sheet, leaving a ½-inch border across the top. Make a ¼-inch deep indentation crosswise along the center of the rice, then spread a thin line of the wasabi paste along the center of the indentation. Top the wasabi paste with one-quarter of the cucumber, avocado, and carrot.

5. Holding the filling in place with your fingers, gently roll the mat forward with your thumbs until the two ends of the nori overlap to form a 7-inch roll. Transfer the roll to a cutting board. With a very sharp knife moistened with water, cut the roll crosswise into four 1½-inch pieces. Repeat with the remaining nori, rice, wasabi paste, cucumber, avocado, and carrot to make eight rolls.

Per serving (2 rolls or 8 pieces): 315 Cal, 7 g Fat, 1 g Sat Fat, 0 mg Chol, 331 mg Sod, 60 g Carb, 7 g Fib, 6 g Prot, 22 mg Calc. *POINTS: 6.*

Tuna Sushi with Soy Dipping Sauce

MAKES 8 SERVINGS

Delicious sushi is great party food and easy to make at home. Just be sure you use only impeccably fresh ingredients. Only buy fish from a reputable fishmonger and ask for "sushi-quality" tuna. Serve sushi with sake, green tea, or slivers of pickled ginger.

5 tablespoons seasoned rice vinegar
3 tablespoons sugar
⅛ teaspoon salt
1⅓ cups sushi or short-grain white rice
1 tablespoon wasabi powder
½ cup reduced-sodium soy sauce
2 tablespoons chopped scallions
1 teaspoon Asian (dark) sesame oil
1 pound tuna fillet, cut into 32 (1 x 3-inch) pieces

1. Heat 3 tablespoons of the vinegar, the sugar, and salt in a small saucepan over medium-low heat until the sugar is dissolved, about 3 minutes. Remove from the heat and cool.
2. Meanwhile, place the rice in a bowl. Add enough water to cover by several inches and gently swish the grains in the bowl with your fingertips, until the water becomes cloudy; drain. Repeat three or four times, until the water is clear. Drain.
3. Combine the rice and 1½ cups fresh water in a medium saucepan; let stand 20 minutes.
4. Bring the rice mixture a boil. Cover, reduce heat to low, and simmer 15 minutes. Remove the saucepan from the heat and let the rice sit undisturbed 10 minutes. Transfer the rice to a large bowl; cool. Stir in the vinegar mixture with a rubber spatula until blended. Cover the rice with a clean, damp kitchen towel; set aside.
5. Whisk the wasabi with 1 tablespoon plus 1 teaspoon warm water, to make a paste. Set aside.
6. To make the dipping sauce, whisk the soy sauce, the remaining 2 tablespoons of the vinegar, the scallions, and sesame oil in a small bowl until blended; set aside.
7. With wet hands, place about 2 tablespoons of the rice in the palm of your hand. Shape the rice into a firm, even oval, about 1½ inches long. Hold the rice in the palm of one hand. Quickly smear one piece of the tuna with a little of the wasabi paste with your other hand. Gently press the tuna, wasabi-side down, onto the rice, cupping your hand to mold the tuna around the rice. Repeat with the remaining rice, wasabi, and tuna to make 32 pieces. Serve the sushi with the dipping sauce.

Per serving (4 pieces with 1 generous tablespoon dipping sauce): 192 Cal, 1 g Fat, 0 g Sat Fat, 26 mg Chol, 851 mg Sod, 27 g Carb, 1 g Fib, 16 g Prot, 17 mg Calc. *POINTS: 4.*

Tuna Sushi with Soy Dipping Sauce

Miso Soup with Spinach and Tofu

MAKES 4 SERVINGS

Many Japanese start their day with a bowl of this healthy and delicious soup. The broth is prepared with dried wakame, edible seaweed with long dark green strands. It is very nutritious and purported to be good for the hair and skin. Wakame requires little cooking time but needs to be soaked for a few minutes with the center rib removed before adding to the soup. Miso, which provides an additional dimension of flavor, is a rich, savory paste made from fermented soybeans. It is also used in salads, marinades, and spreads. Both miso and wakame can be found in health-food stores and Asian groceries.

8 strands dried wakame

4 cups reduced-sodium chicken broth

2 cups baby spinach, cleaned and chopped

¼ pound extra-firm tofu, cut into ¼-inch dice

2 tablespoons miso

1. Place the wakame in a large bowl; add enough hot water to cover. Let stand until the wakame is soft, about 10 minutes; drain. Remove and discard the tough center rib and coarsely chop; set aside.

2. Bring the broth to a boil in a medium saucepan. Add the wakame. Reduce heat to low; cover and simmer until tender, 20 minutes. Add the spinach and tofu. Cook until the spinach just begins to wilt, about 3 minutes. Remove from the heat.

3. Combine ¼ cup of the hot broth with the miso in a small bowl until blended. Stir into the soup. Serve at once.

Per serving (1¼ cups): 88 Cal, 3 g Fat, 1 g Sat Fat, 4 mg Chol, 893 mg Sod, 8 g Carb, 3 g Fib, 8 g Prot, 58 mg Calc. *POINTS: 1.*

the perfect pantry

These are the staples any Japanese cook needs.

- **Japanese eggplant:** Very narrow, straight eggplant; tender, slightly sweet flesh.
- **Japanese seasoned rice vinegar:** Vinegar made from fermented rice seasoned with sugar and salt.
- **Mirin:** Sweet, golden Japanese wine made from glutinous rice.
- **Miso:** Fermented soybean paste; light-colored variety used in delicate soups and sauces, darker variety in heavier dishes.
- **Nori:** Dark green to black paper-thin sheets of dried seaweed; sweet ocean taste.
- **Pickled ginger:** Sliced, fresh ginger preserved in sweet vinegar.
- **Sake:** Japanese wine made from fermented rice; yellowish in color, slightly sweet flavor.
- **Soba:** Japanese noodle made from buckwheat flour.
- **Somen:** Thin white Japanese noodle made from wheat flour.
- **Sushi rice:** Short, fat grains with a higher starch content than long- or medium-grain rice; very moist and viscous when cooked so the grains stick together.

Fiery Tuna and Pea Shoot Salad

MAKES 4 SERVINGS ♦

Pea shoots are the delicate crisp vines and leaves of the young green pea plant. Sweet, tender, and with a strong pea taste, they're wonderful in salads, soups, or tossed into a stir-fry. If pea shoots can't be found at your market or health-food store, substitute broccoli sprouts, radish sprouts, or watercress.

- 1 tablespoon wasabi powder
- 1 tablespoon water
- 1 teaspoon reduced-sodium soy sauce
- 1 pound tuna fillet, cut into 4 equal pieces
- 1 teaspoon canola oil
- 2 tablespoons mirin
- 1 tablespoon seasoned rice vinegar
- 1 tablespoon pickled ginger, finely chopped
- 1 tablespoon pickled ginger juice
- 1 (2-ounce) container pea shoots (about 3 cups)
- 1 small cucumber, peeled and diced (8 ounces)
- 1 cup thinly sliced radishes
- 1 yellow bell pepper, seeded and finely diced
- 3 scallions, thinly sliced

1. Combine the wasabi, water, and soy sauce in a small bowl to make a paste. Pat the tuna dry with a paper towel. Brush both sides of each piece of tuna with the wasabi paste.

2. Heat a medium nonstick skillet over medium–high heat. Swirl in the oil, then add the tuna. Cook until the tuna is browned on the outside and just pink in the center for medium doneness, about 3 minutes on each side. Transfer the tuna to a plate, cover and keep warm.

3. Meanwhile, whisk the mirin, vinegar, pickled ginger, and ginger juice in a small bowl. Combine the pea shoots, cucumber, radishes, bell pepper, and scallions in a large bowl; toss with the dressing to coat well.

4. Divide the salad among 4 serving plates. Top each serving with a piece of tuna.

Per serving (1 piece tuna with 1¼ cups salad): 301 Cal, 3 g Fat, 1 g Sat Fat, 49 mg Chol, 283 mg Sod, 37 g Carb, 6 g Fib, 35 g Prot, 93 mg Calc. *POINTS: 5.*

clever cook's tip

Wasabi, Japanese horseradish, is available in both powder form and as a paste in a squeeze tube. You can purchase wasabi in specialty and Asian markets, as well as in many supermarkets.

Shrimp and Soba Salad

MAKES 4 SERVINGS

Japanese soba are thin buckwheat noodles with a wonderfully robust, earthy flavor. These noodles can be found in health-food stores, Asian groceries, or in the ethnic aisle of your supermarket. Soba are commonly served in a hot, steaming broth, but they also make a terrific Asian-style pasta salad. Whole-wheat spaghetti is an excellent substitute if soba is not readily available in your neighborhood.

1 tablespoon mirin
1 tablespoon seasoned rice vinegar
1 tablespoon reduced-sodium soy sauce
1 tablespoon sugar
1 teaspoon Asian (dark) sesame oil
1 teaspoon minced peeled fresh ginger
1 clove garlic, minced
½ pound soba noodles
4 scallions, thinly sliced
1 carrot, cut into matchstick-thin strips
¼ pound fresh snow peas, trimmed and cut diagonally in half
¾ pound large shrimp, peeled and deveined

1. To make the dressing, whisk the mirin, vinegar, soy sauce, sugar, sesame oil, ginger, and garlic in a small bowl until blended. Set aside.

2. Bring a large pot of water to a boil. Add the noodles and cook until just tender, about 4 minutes. With a strainer or tongs, transfer the noodles to a large bowl of cold water to cool; drain. Reserve the cooking liquid.

3. Transfer the drained noodles to a large bowl. Stir in the scallions and the carrot; set aside.

4. Return the cooking liquid to a boil. Add the snow peas and boil just until bright green and almost tender, about 2 minutes. Transfer the snow peas to a colander with a slotted spoon; rinse under cold water and drain. Add the snow peas to the bowl with the noodles.

5. Cook the shrimp in the same pot of boiling water until just pink, about 3 minutes; drain. Rinse the shrimp under cold water; drain and transfer to the bowl with the noodle mixture. Toss the salad with the dressing to coat well. Serve at room temperature or chilled.

Per serving (1¼ cups): 314 Cal, 2 g Fat, 0 g Sat Fat, 101 mg Chol, 481 mg Sod, 54 g Carb, 3 g Fib, 23 g Prot, 48 mg Calc. **POINTS: 6.**

clever cook's tip

If using whole-wheat spaghetti, cook according to package directions, except transfer the spaghetti with a strainer or tongs to a large bowl of cold water to cool; drain. Reserve the cooking liquid in the pot.

Cold Somen Noodle Salad

MAKES 4 SERVINGS ⏱

A summertime specialty, ultrathin somen noodles are traditionally served cold with a dipping sauce. We tossed the noodles with the sauce instead and added black sesame seeds, frequently used in Japanese cooking (they have a slightly nuttier flavor than their white counterpart). Add strips of cooked skinless chicken or turkey breast if you like.

¼ cup mirin
2 teaspoons seasoned rice vinegar
1 teaspoon reduced-sodium soy sauce
1 teaspoon minced peeled fresh ginger
2 teaspoons black or white sesame seeds, toasted
1 teaspoon Asian (dark) sesame oil
½ pound somen noodles
1 bunch watercress, tough stems removed and coarsely chopped (3 cups)
½ cucumber, peeled and diced (1 cup)
4 scallions, chopped
1 red bell pepper, seeded and diced

1. To make the sauce, whisk the mirin, vinegar, soy sauce, ginger, sesame seeds, and sesame oil in small bowl until blended. Set aside.

2. Bring a large pot of water to a boil. Add the noodles and cook until just tender, about 4 minutes; drain.

3. Transfer the noodles to a large bowl of cold water to cool; drain, then place in a large bowl. Add the watercress, cucumber, scallions, and bell pepper. Stir in the sauce and toss to coat.

Per serving (1½ cups): 365 Cal, 2 g Fat, 0 g Sat Fat, 0 mg Chol, 473 mg Sod, 71 g Carb, 5 g Fib, 11 g Prot, 67 mg Calc. **POINTS: 7.**

beyond sushi

Grilled Sesame Tofu with Sautéed Spinach

MAKES 4 SERVINGS

Everyone knows that tofu is good for you, but it is often thought of as bland and tasteless. The key to working with tofu is understanding that you need to pair it with flavorful ingredients—as we've done in this healthful dish with a lovely soy, sesame, and honey sauce.

3 tablespoons mirin
2 tablespoons reduced-sodium soy sauce
1 teaspoon seasoned rice vinegar
2 teaspoons Asian (dark) sesame oil
¼ cup sesame seeds
2 tablespoons honey
1 (15-ounce) package extra-firm tofu, cut into sixteen ½-inch-thick pieces
1 pound baby spinach, cleaned
1 teaspoon canola oil
2 tablespoons chopped scallions

1. To make the sauce, whisk the mirin, 1 tablespoon of the soy sauce, the vinegar, and 1 teaspoon of the sesame oil in a small bowl until blended; set aside.

2. Place the sesame seeds in a shallow dish. Whisk the honey and the remaining 1 tablespoon of the soy sauce in a small bowl until blended. Brush both sides of the tofu pieces with the honey mixture and then dip into the sesame seeds.

3. Heat a large nonstick skillet over medium–high heat. Swirl in the remaining 1 teaspoon of the sesame oil, then add the spinach. Cook, turning constantly with tongs, until just wilted, about 3 minutes. Transfer spinach to a platter; cover and keep warm.

4. Wipe the skillet clean and heat over medium–high heat. Swirl in the canola oil, then add the tofu. Cook until the pieces begin to brown, about 2 minutes on each side.

5. Arrange the tofu on top of the spinach. Sprinkle with the scallions and drizzle with the sauce. Serve at once.

Per serving (4 slices tofu with ¼ of spinach mixture): 217 Cal, 10 g Fat, 1 g Sat Fat, 0 mg Chol, 435 mg Sod, 21 g Carb, 4 g Fib, 13 g Prot, 166 mg Calc. **POINTS: 4.**

clever cook's tip

Tofu's silken texture is what enables it to absorb the flavors of a recipe's ingredients. To brush the tofu more easily with the honey, heat the honey in the microwave for 10 seconds. Or, place the jar in a small pan with a little simmering water and heat until just warmed and more fluid.

Japanese Eggplant and Tofu in Garlic Sauce

MAKES 4 SERVINGS 🔥 ⏱

Japanese eggplant is smaller and sweeter than the common oblong variety, and the good news is it's now available in most supermarkets. The traditional eggplant is fine to use, however; just cut it into 2-inch pieces before cooking. For a tasty vegetarian entrée, serve this sweet-and-spicy combination over brown rice.

½ cup reduced-sodium chicken broth
¼ cup sake
¼ cup mirin
¼ cup reduced-sodium soy sauce
1 tablespoon minced peeled fresh ginger
3 cloves garlic, minced
1 teaspoon hot chili paste
1 teaspoon cornstarch
1 teaspoon canola oil
6 Japanese eggplants, quartered lengthwise (1 pound)
¼ pound shiitake mushrooms
3 scallions, cut into 3-inch pieces
½ pound extra-firm tofu, cut into 1-inch pieces

1. Whisk the broth, sake, mirin, soy sauce, ginger, garlic, chili paste, and cornstarch in a small bowl until blended. Set aside.

2. Heat a large nonstick skillet over medium-high heat. Swirl in the oil, then add the eggplant. Cook, stirring occasionally, until the eggplant is almost tender, about 8 minutes. Add the mushrooms and scallions. Cook, stirring occasionally, until the vegetables are tender, about 5 minutes. Stir in the tofu; toss gently to combine. Add the broth mixture; bring to a boil. Simmer until the sauce bubbles and begins to thicken slightly, about 3 minutes. Serve at once.

Per serving (1¼ cups): 157 Cal, 4 g Fat, 1 g Sat Fat, 1 mg Chol, 636 mg Sod, 18 g Carb, 3 g Fib, 9 g Prot, 114 mg Calc. ***POINTS: 3.***

Chicken Yakitori

Chicken Yakitori

MAKES 4 SERVINGS

Yakitori are grilled chicken skewers served with a sweet soy-ginger sauce. We think the best part of the chicken to use for yakitori is the moist and tender thigh meat, so look for packages of skinless boneless chicken thighs; they're readily available at the supermarket and cheap, to boot!

¼ cup reduced-sodium soy sauce

2 tablespoons mirin

2 tablespoons sugar

1 teaspoon minced peeled fresh ginger

1 clove garlic

1 pound skinless boneless chicken thighs, trimmed of all visible fat, cut into 2-inch pieces

2 red bell peppers, seeded and cut into 2-inch pieces

8 scallions, cut into 2-inch pieces

2 cups cooked brown rice

1. To make the sauce, bring the soy sauce, mirin, sugar, ginger, and garlic to a boil in a small saucepan. Cook over medium-high heat until the sauce thickens and nicely coats the back of a wooden spoon, about 5 minutes. Remove from the heat; set aside.

2. Spray the grill or broiler pan with nonstick spray; prepare the grill or preheat the broiler.

3. Thread the chicken, bell peppers, and scallions onto each of 8 (10-inch) metal skewers, alternating the ingredients. Grill or broil the kebabs 5 inches from the heat, frequently brushing with the sauce, until the vegetables are tender and the chicken is cooked through, about 10 minutes. Serve with the rice.

Per serving (2 skewers with ½ cup rice): 364 Cal, 10 g Fat, 3 g Sat Fat, 81 mg Chol, 686 mg Sod, 39 g Carb, 4 g Fib, 26 g Prot, 45 mg Calc.
POINTS: 7.

clever cook's tip

Metal skewers can become extremely hot on the grill, so use tongs or hot pads when transferring the skewers to the serving plates.

Chicken-Vegetable Udon

MAKES 6 SERVINGS

This big bowl of thick wheat noodles and vegetables in a fragrant broth is Japan's answer to comfort food. Our version includes thin strips of chicken poached in a delicate blend of soy sauce, sake, garlic, and ginger.

¼ **pound udon noodles (or spaghetti, cooked according to package directions)**

1 **teaspoon canola oil**

1 **tablespoon minced peeled fresh ginger**

2 **cloves garlic, minced**

4 **cups reduced-sodium chicken broth**

3 **tablespoons sake**

2 **tablespoons reduced-sodium soy sauce**

4 **(¼-pound) skinless boneless chicken breasts, cut into ½-inch-thick strips**

1 **cup shiitake mushrooms, sliced (4 ounces)**

6 **scallions, chopped**

1 **carrot, cut diagonally into thin slices**

¼ **cup fresh cilantro leaves**

1. Bring a large pot of water to a boil. Add the noodles and cook until tender, about 20 minutes; drain.

2. Meanwhile, heat a large saucepan over medium-high heat. Swirl in the oil, then add the ginger and garlic. Cook, stirring, until fragrant, about 30 seconds. Add the chicken, stirring to coat. Stir in the broth, sake, and soy sauce; bring to a simmer. Cover and cook at a gentle simmer until the chicken is cooked through, about 10 minutes. Add the mushrooms, scallions, and carrot. Cover and simmer until the vegetables are tender, about 5 minutes. Stir in the noodles and sprinkle with the cilantro leaves.

Per serving (1 generous cup): 183 Cal, 4 g Fat, 1 g Sat Fat, 44 mg Chol, 433 mg Sod, 16 g Carb, 1 g Fib, 20 g Prot, 36 mg Calc. ***POINTS: 4.***

clever cook's tip

If you have access to an Asian-specialty market, look for fresh udon noodles. They're delicious and only take 3 to 5 minutes to cook.

Teriyaki Tuna with Ginger Vegetables

MAKES 4 SERVINGS

Teriyaki is perhaps the most popular dish for Japanese take-out. But once you see just how easy it is to throw together, you'll be tempted to make it at home more often. While beef, chicken, or salmon teriyaki are familiar choices, it's especially delicious with fresh tuna—which adapts beautifully to the sweet soy-based sauce. Although there are many commercial brands of teriyaki sauce available, our version is ready in a flash and tastes far less salty.

¼ cup reduced-sodium soy sauce

¼ cup sake

2 tablespoons mirin

1 tablespoon sugar

1 teaspoon canola oil

1 tablespoon minced peeled fresh ginger

2 cloves garlic, minced

1 red bell pepper, seeded and thinly sliced

1 yellow bell pepper, seeded and thinly sliced

1 cup fresh snow peas, trimmed and halved on the diagonal

1 carrot, cut into matchstick-thin strips

1 pound tuna fillet, cut into 4 equal pieces

1. To make the sauce, bring the soy sauce, sake, mirin, and sugar to a boil in a small saucepan. Cook over medium-high heat until the sauce is thickened and reduced by half (¼ cup), about 5 minutes. Remove the sauce from the heat. Transfer half the sauce to a bowl; cover and keep warm.

2. Spray the broiler or grill rack with nonstick spray; preheat the broiler or prepare the grill.

3. Heat a large nonstick skillet over medium-high heat. Swirl in the oil, then add the ginger and garlic. Cook, stirring, until fragrant, less than 1 minute. Add the bell peppers, snow peas, and carrots; cook, stirring, until the vegetables are tender-crisp, 4–5 minutes.

4. Meanwhile, broil or grill the tuna 5 inches from the heat, turning occasionally and brushing with half of the sauce, until golden brown and just slightly pink in the center, about 3 minutes on each side.

5. Divide the vegetable mixture among 4 plates. Top each serving with a piece of tuna and drizzle with the remaining sauce. Serve at once.

Per serving (1 piece tuna with ½ cup vegetables): 216 Cal, 2 g Fat, 0 g Sat Fat, 49 mg Chol, 658 mg Sod, 17 g Carb, 3 g Fib, 29 g Prot, 49 mg Calc. *POINTS: 4.*

clever cook's tip

If you love to grill, make a big batch of teriyaki sauce to use with meat, poultry, or even vegetables. It will keep indefinitely in the refrigerator.

beyond sushi

Scallops and Asparagus with Sake

MAKES 4 SERVINGS

Sake, an alcoholic beverage made from steamed fermented rice, is colorless (or very pale yellow) and slightly sweet. Sake is traditionally served warm in small porcelain cups, but it's also excellent in marinades and sauces—as evident in this delicious scallop entrée.

- 2 teaspoons canola oil
- 1 pound sea scallops, muscle removed
- 2 teaspoons minced peeled fresh ginger
- 2 cloves garlic, minced
- ½ pound asparagus, cut diagonally into 1½-inch pieces
- 1 red bell pepper, seeded and thinly sliced
- 1 yellow bell pepper, seeded and thinly sliced
- 1 carrot, cut into matchstick-thin strips
- 2 tablespoons sake
- 1 tablespoon reduced-sodium soy sauce
- 1 teaspoon seasoned rice vinegar
- 4 scallions, thinly sliced diagonally

1. Heat a large nonstick skillet over medium-high heat. Swirl in 1 teaspoon of the oil, then add the scallops. Cook, turning, until golden brown on the outside and just opaque in the center, about 1 minute on each side. Transfer the scallops to a plate, cover and keep warm.

2. Return the pan to the heat. Swirl in the remaining 1 teaspoon oil, then add the ginger and the garlic. Cook, stirring, until fragrant, less than 1 minute. Add the asparagus, bell peppers, and carrot; cook, stirring, until the vegetables are tender-crisp, 3–4 minutes.

3. Stir in the sake, soy sauce, and vinegar; bring to a boil. Cook over high heat, stirring, until the flavors are blended. Return the scallops to the pan; stir in the scallions. Cook until just heated through. Serve at once.

Per serving: 124 Cal, 4 g Fat, 0 g Sat Fat, 18 mg Chol, 297 mg Sod, 11 g Carb, 2 g Fib, 11 g Prot, 43 mg Calc. ***POINTS: 2.***

clever cook's tip

If fresh asparagus aren't available, try green beans or peas. If you use fresh peas, stir them in at the end with the scallions.

Scallops and
Asparagus with Sake

6

now, that's italian!

Antipasto Platter

A sumptuous antipasto platter such as this embodies Italian cuisine today, just as it has for centuries. Anchovy lovers can sprinkle 3 chopped drained anchovies over their portion of this tempting array and add an extra ½ **POINT.** To make ahead, marinate the artichoke hearts in the refrigerator for up to 2 days, then assemble the remaining ingredients just before serving. *Mangia bene!*

2 tablespoons balsamic vinegar

1 tablespoon extra-virgin olive oil

1 garlic clove, minced

½ teaspoon freshly ground pepper

1 (9-ounce) package frozen artichoke hearts, cooked and drained

12 thin slices prosciutto (about ¼ pound)

½ cantaloupe, peeled and cut into 12 short wedges

2 ounces fresh mozzarella cheese, cut into ½-inch cubes

½ fennel bulb, thinly sliced

2 plum tomatoes, sliced

10 fresh basil leaves, cut into thin strips

12 kalamata olives

6 ounces Italian bread, cut into 12 slices and toasted

1. Combine the vinegar, oil, garlic, and pepper in a medium bowl. Add the artichoke hearts while still warm; toss to coat. Set aside to blend the flavors, about 10 minutes.

2. Wrap the prosciutto slices around the cantaloupe wedges; secure with toothpicks.

3. Drain the artichoke hearts, reserving the dressing; place at one end of a large platter. Arrange the prosciutto-wrapped melon at the other end, and the mozzarella, fennel, and tomatoes in the middle. Sprinkle the reserved dressing and the basil over the cheese, fennel, and tomatoes. Sprinkle with the olives and serve with the toasts.

Per serving (¹⁄₁₂ of platter): 118 Cal, 5 g Fat, 2 g Sat Fat, 10 mg Chol, 401 mg Sod, 13 g Carb, 2 g Fib, 6 g Prot, 54 mg Calc. **POINTS: 2.**

clever cook's tip

You can transform this recipe into a picnic lunch for six by storing the ingredients in separate zip-close plastic bags, then assembling on-site. For best flavor, use prosciutto imported from Italy, such as prosciutto di Parma.

Bruschetta with Red Pepper Pesto

MAKES 8 SERVINGS

This recipe is a party-perfect starter. You can prepare the Red Pepper Pesto ahead of time. Simply keep it covered in the refrigerator for up to 3 days.

- 2 red bell peppers, seeded and quartered
- 1 cup lightly packed fresh basil leaves
- 2 garlic cloves, sliced
- 2 tablespoons pine nuts, toasted
- 2 teaspoons extra-virgin olive oil
- ¼ teaspoon salt
- ¼ teaspoon freshly ground pepper
- 1 (12-ounce) Italian semolina bread, cut into 24 slices and toasted
- 1 ounce Parmesan cheese, shaved

1. Preheat the broiler. Line a baking sheet with foil; place the bell peppers on the baking sheet. Broil 5 inches from the heat, turning occasionally with tongs, until lightly charred, about 10 minutes. Let cool slightly.

2. Thinly slice ¼ cup of the basil leaves; set aside for garnish. Puree the bell peppers, the remaining ¾ cup basil, the garlic, pine nuts, oil, salt, and pepper in a blender or food processor. Transfer the pesto to a small bowl.

3. Spread 1 scant tablespoon of the pesto on each toast slice; top with a few of the reserved sliced basil leaves and a shaving or two of the Parmesan.

Per serving (3 toasts): 176 Cal, 5 g Fat, 1 g Sat Fat, 3 mg Chol, 413 mg Sod, 26 g Carb, 2 g Fib, 7 g Prot, 98 mg Calc. **POINTS: 4.**

clever cook's tip

This pesto is also delicious tossed with your favorite pasta. For four servings, toss 4 cups cooked pasta with about ½ cup of the pesto.

now, that's italian!

Focaccia with Pesto and Sun-Dried Tomatoes

MAKES 16 SERVINGS

Focaccia is a flat bread or a thick pizza with fewer toppings. This hearty bread is ideal served with Minestrone [page 145] or another favorite soup on a chilly day. If you have a baking or pizza stone, preheat it and bake the focaccia on it—this will help produce a crisper crust.

1 **cup warm (105 °F–115 °F) water**
1 **teaspoon sugar**
1 **package active dry yeast**
2¼ **cups all-purpose flour**
¼ **cup toasted wheat germ**
½ **teaspoon salt**
2 **tablespoons cornmeal**
2 **tablespoons prepared pesto**
¼ **cup oil-packed sun-dried tomatoes, drained, patted dry with paper towels, and chopped**
¼ **cup grated Pecorino Romano cheese**

1. Combine the water and sugar in a small bowl. Sprinkle in the yeast and let stand until foamy, about 5 minutes.

2. Combine the flour, wheat germ, and salt in a food processor. With the machine running, scrape the yeast mixture through the feed tube; pulse until the dough forms a smooth ball, about 1 minute.

3. Spray a large bowl with nonstick spray; put the dough in the bowl. Cover tightly with plastic wrap and let the dough rise in a warm, draft-free place until it doubles in size, about 1 hour.

4. Spray a nonstick baking sheet with nonstick spray; sprinkle with the cornmeal.

5. Punch down the dough. Sprinkle a work surface lightly with flour. Turn the dough onto the surface; knead lightly into a ball. With a lightly floured rolling pin, roll dough into a 12-inch circle. Transfer the dough to the baking sheet, gently stretching the dough back into a 12-inch circle. Make dimples all over the dough with a wooden spoon handle, then prick all over with the tines of a fork. Spread with the pesto, then sprinkle with the sun-dried tomatoes and Romano. Let rise in a warm, draft-free place, about 40 minutes.

6. Preheat the oven to 425° F. Bake the focaccia until the crust is golden and crisp around the edges, about 18 minutes. Cool on the baking sheet on a rack 5 minutes. To serve, slide the focaccia onto a large cutting board, then cut into 16 slices.

Per serving (1 slice): 96 Cal, 2 g Fat, 1 g Sat Fat, 2 mg Chol, 112 mg Sod, 16 g Carb, 1 g Fib, 4 g Prot, 35 mg Calc. ***POINTS: 2.***

Pepperoni-Mushroom Pizza

MAKES 6 SERVINGS

Pepperoni pizza has long been a favorite for many of us, and we've come up with a satisfying 6-*POINT* substitute made with turkey pepperoni—which is every bit as flavorful as beef or pork pepperoni but has much less fat. Turkey pepperoni comes in packages of small, thin slices, perfect for topping a pizza. If you have an abundance of fresh tomatoes, substitute 2 large tomatoes, sliced, for the cup of marinara sauce.

2 tablespoons cornmeal

1 tablespoon olive oil

¼ pound white mushrooms, sliced

1 (15-ounce) package refrigerated pizza dough, at room temperature

1 cup prepared marinara sauce

½ cup shredded part-skim mozzarella cheese

2 ounces (from a 6-ounce package) thinly sliced, ready-to-eat turkey pepperoni

1. Adjust the oven racks to divide the oven into thirds. Preheat the oven to 450° F. Spray a nonstick baking sheet with nonstick spray; sprinkle with the cornmeal.

2. Heat a medium nonstick skillet over medium-high heat. Swirl in the oil, then add the mushrooms. Cook, stirring occasionally, until lightly browned, about 5 minutes.

3. Punch down the dough. Sprinkle a work surface lightly with flour. Turn the dough onto the surface; knead lightly into a ball. With a lightly floured rolling pin, roll dough into a 12-inch circle. Transfer the dough to the baking sheet, gently stretching the dough back into a 12-inch circle; prick all over with a fork. Bake on the lowest oven rack 5 minutes.

4. Spoon the marinara sauce onto crust, then sprinkle with the mozzarella. Top with the mushrooms and pepperoni slices. Bake on the lowest rack until the crust is browned and the cheese is melted, about 15 minutes longer. To serve, slide the pizza onto a large cutting board and then cut into 6 slices.

Per serving (1 slice): 293 Cal, 8 g Fat, 6 g Sat Fat, 17 mg Chol, 865 mg Sod, 41 g Carb, 2 g Fib, 13 g Prot, 73 mg Calc. *POINTS: 6.*

clever cook's tip

Baking the unadorned crust for 5 minutes makes it crispy. If the crust puffs up a little, simply prick it again with a fork to deflate it.

Pizza Margherita

MAKES 4 SERVINGS

Simplicity and light toppings are the secret to this classic pizza. Rather than being laden with sauce and cheese, it's topped with lightly cooked onions, fresh tomatoes, and just a touch of mozzarella. Also, the crust is prebaked to make the finished pizza crispy.

½ cup + 1 tablespoon warm (105° F–115° F) water
½ teaspoon sugar
1 package active dry yeast
1¼ cups all-purpose flour
¼ cup whole-wheat flour
¼ teaspoon salt
2 teaspoons olive oil
1 onion, chopped
2 garlic cloves, minced
6 plum tomatoes, chopped
¼ teaspoon coarsely ground black pepper
2 tablespoons cornmeal
¼ cup grated Parmesan cheese
2 ounces part-skim mozzarella cheese, thinly sliced
10 fresh basil leaves, thinly sliced

1. Combine the water and sugar in a small bowl. Sprinkle in the yeast and let stand until foamy, about 5 minutes.
2. Combine the all-purpose flour, whole-wheat flour, and salt in a food processor. With the machine running, scrape the yeast mixture through the feed tube; pulse until the dough forms a smooth ball, about 1 minute.
3. Spray a large bowl with nonstick spray; put the dough in the bowl. Cover tightly with plastic wrap and let the dough rise in a warm, draft-free place until it doubles in size, about 1 hour.
4. Meanwhile, heat a large nonstick saucepan over medium-high heat. Swirl in the oil, then add the onion and garlic. Cook, stirring occasionally, until golden, 7–10 minutes. Add the tomatoes and pepper; cook until softened, 3–5 minutes. Remove from the heat and set aside.
5. Adjust the oven racks to divide the oven into thirds. Preheat the oven to 500° F. Spray a nonstick baking sheet with nonstick spray; sprinkle with the cornmeal.
6. Punch down the dough. Sprinkle a work surface lightly with flour. Turn the dough onto the surface, knead lightly into a ball. With a lightly floured rolling pin, roll dough into a 12-inch circle. Transfer the dough to the baking sheet, gently stretching the dough back into a 12-inch circle. Sprinkle with the Parmesan; let rest 10 minutes. Bake on the lowest oven rack until lightly browned and crisp, about 8 minutes.
7. Spoon the tomato mixture onto the baked pizza crust; top with the mozzarella and bake until hot and the cheese melts, 5–6 minutes longer. To serve, slide the pizza onto a large cutting board, sprinkle with the basil, and cut into 4 slices.

Per serving (1 slice): 309 Cal, 8 g Fat, 3 g Sat Fat, 13 mg Chol, 348 mg Sod, 47 g Carb, 4 g Fib, 14 g Prot, 214 mg Calc. **POINTS: 6.**

Pizza with the Works and
Pizza Margherita (below)

Pizza with the Works

MAKES 6 SERVINGS

You want it all? Make this take-out favorite our way, and you can have it—without blowing the **POINTS** bank. Serve with a large green salad sprinkled with good balsamic vinegar.

2 teaspoons olive oil

1 onion, thinly sliced

¼ pound sweet Italian turkey sausage, casings removed and crumbled

1 red bell pepper, seeded and thinly sliced

1 green bell pepper, seeded and thinly sliced

¼ pound cremini mushrooms, sliced

2 plum tomatoes, sliced

1 (10-ounce) package thin pizza crust

1 tablespoon capers, rinsed and drained

1 cup shredded part-skim mozzarella cheese

2 tablespoons shredded Parmesan cheese

2 anchovy fillets, rinsed and chopped

1. Preheat the oven to 450° F. Heat a 12- to 14-inch nonstick skillet over medium-high heat. Swirl in the oil, then add the onion. Cook, stirring frequently, until softened, about 3 minutes. Add the sausage and bell peppers. Cook, stirring occasionally, until the sausage is browned and the bell peppers are slightly softened, 6–8 minutes. Add the mushrooms and tomatoes. Cook, stirring occasionally, until softened and the juices are released, about 4 minutes.

2. Place the pizza crust on a baking sheet. Spread the sausage mixture on the crust. Sprinkle with the capers, mozzarella, and Parmesan. Bake until hot and the cheeses are lightly browned, 8–10 minutes. To serve, slide the pizza onto a large cutting board, sprinkle with the anchovies, then cut into 6 slices.

Per serving (1 slice): 290 Cal, 13 g Fat, 4 g Sat Fat, 24 mg Chol, 550 mg Sod, 29 g Carb, 2 g Fib, 14 g Prot, 187 mg Calc. **POINTS: 6.**

clever cook's tip

For a crispier crust, use a baking or pizza stone. Remember to preheat it in the oven for 20 minutes before you use it. If you don't own a pizza stone, use your darkest baking sheet (it helps produce a crispier crust).

Vegetable Calzones

MAKES 6 SERVINGS

Simple turnovers made from pizza dough, calzones are traditionally filled with an abundance of mozzarella and salami. Here we use less cheese and add flavorful, crunchy vegetables to make a delicious portable meal suitable for a quick office lunch.

¾ **cup warm (105° F–115° F) water**

1 **teaspoon sugar**

1 **package active dry yeast**

2 **cups all-purpose flour**

½ **cup whole-wheat flour**

¾ **teaspoon salt**

1 **large egg**

1 **cup shredded part-skim mozzarella cheese**

¾ **cup part-skim ricotta cheese**

2 **plum tomatoes, chopped**

½ **green bell pepper, seeded and diced**

3 **scallions, thinly sliced**

2 **tablespoons chopped fresh basil**

¼ **teaspoon freshly ground pepper**

1. Combine the water and sugar in a small bowl. Sprinkle in the yeast and let stand until foamy, about 5 minutes.

2. Combine the all-purpose flour, whole-wheat flour, and salt in a food processor. With the machine running, scrape the yeast mixture and the egg through the feed tube; pulse until the dough forms a smooth ball, about 1 minute.

3. Spray a large bowl with nonstick spray; put the dough in the bowl. Cover tightly with plastic wrap and let the dough rise in a warm, draft-free place until it doubles in size, about 1 hour.

4. Meanwhile, combine the mozzarella, ricotta, tomatoes, bell pepper, scallions, basil, and pepper in a medium bowl.

5. Preheat the oven to 400° F. Spray a baking sheet with nonstick spray; set aside.

6. Punch down the dough. Sprinkle a work surface lightly with flour. Turn the dough onto the surface and cut into 6 pieces. Knead each piece lightly, then with a lightly floured rolling pin, roll each into a 6-inch circle. Mound one-sixth of the cheese mixture on half of each circle, then brush the edges lightly with water. Fold the dough over the filling; crimp the edges to seal. Transfer the calzones to the baking sheet; make three 1-inch slashes on top of each with a sharp knife. Bake until golden, 20–23 minutes.

Per serving (1 calzone): 304 Cal, 7 g Fat, 4 g Sat Fat, 56 mg Chol, 432 mg Sod, 45 g Carb, 3 g Fib, 16 g Prot, 228 mg Calc. **POINTS: 6.**

Roasted Vegetable Panini

MAKES 4 SERVINGS

More and more popular as a take-out lunch favorite, panini, or small breads, are simply thin grilled sandwiches. Substitute slices of eggplant or portobello mushrooms for any of the vegetables, if you prefer. For convenience, buy presliced provolone; for the best flavor, buy sharp provolone and slice it yourself.

1 red bell pepper, seeded and cut into eighths
1 yellow bell pepper, seeded and cut into eighths
1 medium zucchini, sliced on the diagonal
½ cup thinly sliced fennel
1 small red onion, cut into 8 slices
1 tablespoon chopped fresh rosemary, or 1 teaspoon dried
1 tablespoon extra-virgin olive oil
1 tablespoon balsamic vinegar
¾ teaspoon salt
8 ounces semolina bread, sliced lengthwise into fourths, then cut in half crosswise
4 (1-ounce) slices provolone cheese

1. Preheat the oven to 425° F. Spray a large shallow roasting pan with nonstick spray.

2. Combine the bell peppers, zucchini, fennel, onion, rosemary, oil, vinegar, and salt in a large bowl; toss to coat. Spread the vegetables in one layer in the roasting pan. Roast, stirring occasionally, until the vegetables are tender and browned, 20–25 minutes. Let cool slightly.

3. Spoon about ¾ cup of the vegetable mixture onto one piece of the bread, top with a slice of provolone, then another slice of the bread. Repeat using the remaining vegetables, cheese, and bread, making a total of 4 sandwiches.

4. Lightly spray a nonstick skillet with nonstick spray and set over medium-high heat. Add the sandwiches, two at a time, and top with a heavy weight, such as a cast-iron skillet. Cook until the bread is lightly browned and crisp, about 2 minutes. With a spatula, turn the sandwiches, weigh them down, and cook until the other sides are browned, about 2 minutes. Repeat with the remaining sandwiches.

Per serving (1 panini): 324 Cal, 13 g Fat, 5 g Sat Fat, 20 mg Chol, 1,071 mg Sod, 38 g Carb, 4 g Fib, 14 g Prot, 273 mg Calc. **POINTS: 7.**

clever cook's tip

For a picnic treat, assemble the sandwiches, without toasting them, on-site. The vegetables can be made ahead and refrigerated for up to 2 days. Allow them to come to room temperature and spoon them onto crusty bread rolls layered with cheese.

the perfect pantry

Great Italian cooking is simple if you keep these basics on hand.

- **Arborio rice:** Italian short-grain rice traditionally used for risotto because its high starch content contributes to the creamy texture of the dish.
- **Arugula:** Mildly bitter, aromatic salad green; peppery mustard flavor.
- **Asiago cheese:** Firm Italian grating cheese; rich, nutty taste; made from whole or part-skim cow's milk.
- **Balsamic vinegar:** Italian aged dark vinegar; deep, rich flavor with touch of sweetness.
- **Basil:** Fresh herb commonly used in Italian cooking; pungent flavor that's a cross between licorice and cloves.
- **Broccoli rabe:** Pungent, bitter green with tiny broccoli-like buds.
- **Capers:** Tiny, piquant-tasting buds pickled in vinegar; native to the Mediterranean.
- **Cremini mushrooms:** Dark-brown firmer variation of white mushrooms; slightly fuller flavor than white counterpart.
- **Ditalini:** Tiny short tubes of macaroni.
- **Escarole:** Mild-tasting variety of endive; broad, curved pale green leaves.
- **Extra-virgin olive oil:** Oil produced from first pressing of olives; low acidity; rich, deep, olive flavor; color can range from greenish golden to bright green.
- **Fennel bulb:** Sweet, mild anise-flavored vegetable that can be eaten raw in salads or cooked.
- **Fusilli:** Spiraled spaghetti that can range from 1½ to 12 inches long.
- **Italian plum tomatoes:** Flavorful egg-shaped tomato commonly used both raw and cooked in Italian dishes.
- **Marsala:** Fortified wine from Sicily; rich, smoky flavor ranges from sweet to dry.
- **Mozzarella cheese:** Mild cow's milk-cheese; available in two varieties: factory-produced whole milk, part-skim, or nonfat mozzarella and fresh mozzarella packaged in whey or water, made from whole milk, with a softer texture and a sweet delicate flavor.
- **Pancetta:** Flavorful, slightly salty Italian bacon cured with salt and spices but not smoked.
- **Parmesan cheese:** Italian hard, dry cheese made from skimmed or partially skimmed cow's milk; superior texture and rich, sharp flavor; often aged two years.
- **Pecorino Romano cheese:** Firm, sharp, tangy cheese; made from sheep's milk.
- **Penne:** Medium-size straight tubes of macaroni cut on the diagonal.
- **Pesto:** Classic uncooked fresh basil sauce with garlic, pine nuts, Parmesan cheese, and olive oil.
- **Pine nuts (pignoli):** Small oval-shaped nuts commonly used in sweet and savory Italian dishes.
- **Portobello mushrooms:** Meaty-textured variety of white mushrooms; diameter of mushroom caps can reach up to 6 inches.
- **Prosciutto:** Ham that has been seasoned, salt-cured (but not smoked), and air-dried.
- **Provolone cheese:** Southern Italian cow's-milk cheese; firm texture; mild, smoky flavor.
- **Radicchio:** Red-leaf Italian chicory; most often used in salads.
- **Ricotta cheese:** Moist, slightly grainy fresh cow's-milk cheese with a slightly sweet taste.
- **Sun-dried tomato:** Chewy, intensely flavored dried tomatoes; sweet flavor; either packed in oil or dry-packed in clear packages.

now, that's italian!

Eggplant Parmesan Hero

Eggplant Parmesan Hero

MAKES 4 SERVINGS

A favorite Italian treat, our hero is kept low in **POINTS** by spraying the eggplant with nonstick spray and baking it. For best flavor, use olive oil spray.

1 (1-pound) eggplant, unpeeled and cut into ¼-inch-thick slices

1 large egg

1 tablespoon fat-free milk

½ cup Italian-seasoned dried bread crumbs

2 tablespoons grated Parmesan cheese

¼ cup shredded part-skim mozzarella cheese

1 cup prepared marinara sauce, heated

4 Italian hard rolls, split

1. Preheat the oven to 375° F. Spray a nonstick baking sheet with nonstick spray; set aside.

2. Lightly beat the egg and milk in a shallow bowl. Mix the bread crumbs and Parmesan on a sheet of wax paper. Dip the eggplant in the egg mixture, then in the bread crumbs, and arrange in one layer on the baking sheet. Lightly spray the eggplant with nonstick spray. Bake until the eggplant is softened and lightly browned, about 25 minutes.

3. Divide eggplant slices into 4 equal portions on the baking sheet. Overlap each group of slices so they are no larger than the dimensions of each roll. Top each portion with 1 tablespoon of the mozzarella. Bake until the cheese is melted, about 2 minutes.

4. Transfer each eggplant portion to the bottom of each roll; top each with ¼ cup of the sauce. Replace top of rolls and serve at once.

Per serving (1 hero): 338 Cal, 8 g Fat, 2 g Sat Fat, 60 mg Chol, 796 mg Sod, 53 g Carb, 5 g Fib, 14 g Prot, 204 mg Calc. **POINTS: 7.**

clever cook's tip

For extra flavor (and 1 **POINT** more per serving), spread each roll with ½ tablespoon prepared kalamata olive spread. You can find it in 7- to 8-ounce jars in most large supermarkets.

now, that's italian!

Tricolor Salad with Caper Dressing

MAKES 4 SERVINGS 🕐

For a heartier salad (and an extra 2 **POINTS** per serving), sprinkle each salad with ¾ ounce crumbled reduced-fat goat cheese just before serving and omit the salt.

2 tablespoons balsamic vinegar
1 tablespoon extra-virgin olive oil
1 tablespoon chopped drained capers
1 tablespoon chopped red onion
¼ teaspoon salt
¼ teaspoon freshly ground pepper
1 head radicchio, cleaned and torn
1 bunch arugula, cleaned and torn
1 head Belgian endive, cleaned

Combine the vinegar, oil, capers, onion, salt, and pepper in a large salad bowl. Add the radicchio, arugula, and endive; toss to coat. Serve at once.

Per serving (2 cups): 50 Cal, 4 g Fat, 0 g Sat Fat, 0 mg Chol, 241 mg Sod, 4 g Carb, 1 g Fib, 1 g Prot, 43 mg Calc. **POINTS: 1.**

clever cook's tip

Purchasing prebagged and washed salad greens at your local supermarket makes this recipe an anytime favorite.

Minestrone

MAKES 6 SERVINGS

Hearty enough to be considered a complete meal, Minestrone has been served for years to families of many ethnic backgrounds across this country. Serve with Focaccia with Pesto and Sun-Dried Tomatoes [page 134] or with chunks of semolina bread to round out the meal.

- 2 teaspoons olive oil
- 1 large onion, chopped
- 2 garlic cloves, minced
- 4 cups low-sodium chicken broth
- 1 (28-ounce) can Italian plum tomatoes, cut up
- ½ cup ditalini
- 2 carrots, diced
- 2 celery stalks, diced
- 1 large all-purpose potato, diced
- 1 bunch escarole, cleaned and chopped
- 1 (19-ounce) can cannellini (white kidney) beans, rinsed and drained
- 2 tablespoons fresh oregano leaves, minced, or 2 teaspoons dried
- ¼ teaspoon coarsely ground black pepper
- ¼ cup grated Parmesan cheese

1. Heat a nonstick Dutch oven over medium–high heat. Swirl in the oil, then add the onion and garlic. Cook, stirring occasionally, until golden, 7–10 minutes. Add the broth, tomatoes, ditalini, carrots, celery, and potato; bring to a boil, stirring occasionally. Reduce the heat and simmer, covered, stirring occasionally, until the ditalini and vegetables are just tender, about 20 minutes.

2. Stir in the escarole, beans, oregano, and pepper; return to a boil, stirring occasionally. Reduce the heat and simmer, covered, until the escarole is wilted and softened, 3–4 minutes. Serve with the Parmesan.

Per serving (scant 2 cups): 230 Cal, 4 g Fat, 2 g Sat Fat, 6 mg Chol, 525 mg Sod, 37 g Carb, 9 g Fib, 11 g Prot, 186 mg Calc. *POINTS: 4.*

clever cook's tip

For true Italian flavor, add a bit of the Parmesan cheese rind to the minestrone while it simmers. Substitute 1 (10-ounce) package frozen peas or frozen chopped spinach for the escarole, if you prefer.

Scampi

MAKES 4 SERVINGS

A favorite take-out or eat-in dish, scampi is often dripping in butter. This recipe allows for just enough butter to carry the flavors of the shallot, garlic, and lemon. Our great-taste secret? Make sure to pat the shrimp completely dry with paper towels before tossing them with the butter mixture. This will encourage them to brown, rather than steam, when they are broiled. Serve with boiled red-skinned potatoes, a tossed leafy green salad, and fresh figs for dessert.

4 teaspoons butter
1 shallot, chopped
3 garlic cloves, minced
1 tablespoon fresh lemon juice
½ teaspoon salt
½ teaspoon coarsely ground black pepper
1 pound large shrimp peeled, butterflied, and deveined
2 tablespoons chopped fresh flat-leaf parsley
Lemon wedges

1. Preheat the broiler. Melt the butter in a large nonstick skillet over medium heat, then add the shallot and garlic. Cook, stirring frequently, until golden, 4–5 minutes. Remove from the heat; stir in the lemon juice, salt, and pepper. Add the shrimp and toss to coat.

2. Spread the shrimp in a shallow flameproof baking dish large enough to hold the shrimp in a single layer. Broil 3–4 inches from the heat, until the shrimp are just opaque in the center and lightly browned on the outside, about 3 minutes on each side. Sprinkle with the parsley and serve with the lemon wedges.

Per serving (6 shrimp): 111 Cal, 5 g Fat, 3 g Sat Fat, 145 mg Chol, 448 mg Sod, 2 g Carb, 0 g Fib, 15 g Prot, 38 mg Calc. *POINTS: 3.*

clever cook's tip

Butterflying the shrimp exposes more surface area of the seafood to absorb more flavors from the sauce. Here's how you do it: Peel the shrimp. Then, using a paring knife, slice along the back from top to tail, cutting the shrimp almost, but not entirely, in half. With the blade of your knife, scrape out the vein and slightly flatten the shrimp.

Lobster fra Diavolo

MAKES 6 SERVINGS

Lobster, king of the crustacean family, is perfect in this spicy tomato sauce. Lobster meat is available frozen or canned, but for best results, use fresh lobster tails. To remove the meat from the lobster tail, cut away the soft undercover with scissors, and with your fingers, ease away the meat from the shell.

1 tablespoon olive oil
2 onions, chopped
4 garlic cloves, chopped
1 (28-ounce) can Italian plum tomatoes, cut up
1 yellow bell pepper, seeded and chopped
⅓ cup dry white wine
½ teaspoon crushed red pepper
¼ teaspoon salt
¼ teaspoon coarsely ground black pepper
¾ pound fusilli
3 (½-pound) lobster tails, meat removed and cut into ½-inch pieces
¼ cup chopped fresh basil

1. Heat a large nonstick skillet over medium-high heat. Swirl in the oil, then add the onions and garlic. Cook, stirring occasionally, until golden, 7–10 minutes. Add the tomatoes, bell pepper, wine, crushed red pepper, salt, and pepper; bring to a boil. Reduce the heat and simmer, uncovered, until the flavors are blended and the sauce is slightly thickened, about 20 minutes.

2. Meanwhile, cook the fusilli according to package directions; drain and keep warm in a large bowl.

3. Add the lobster to the sauce and simmer, uncovered, until the lobster is just opaque, about 5 minutes.

4. Toss the lobster sauce with the fusilli and sprinkle with the basil.

Per serving (scant 2 cups): 363 Cal, 5 g Fat, 1 g Sat Fat, 43 mg Chol, 565 mg Sod, 57 g Carb, 5 g Fib, 21 g Prot, 88 mg Calc. *POINTS: 7.*

now, that's italian!

Osso Buco with Gremolata

MAKES 4 SERVINGS

Gremolata—a garnish made from a lively mix of parsley, grated lemon rind, and garlic—adds tangy flavor to this savory stew. Traditionally served with risotto, Osso Buco is also excellent paired with fettuccine or baked russet potatoes.

2 teaspoons olive oil

4 (½-pound) veal shanks, trimmed of all visible fat

2 onions, chopped

3 garlic cloves

½ fennel bulb, chopped

2 carrots, chopped

¾ cup low-sodium chicken broth

⅓ cup dry red wine

2 plum tomatoes, chopped

2 bay leaves

½ teaspoon salt

¼ teaspoon coarsely ground black pepper

2 tablespoons all-purpose flour

2 tablespoons cold water

1 tablespoon finely chopped fresh rosemary, thyme, or sage

⅓ cup chopped fresh flat-leaf parsley

2 tablespoons grated lemon rind

1. Heat a nonstick Dutch oven over medium-high heat. Swirl in the oil, then add the veal shanks. Cook until browned, about 3 minutes on each side. Transfer the veal to a plate and set aside.

2. Mince 2 of the garlic cloves. Add the onions and the minced garlic to the Dutch oven. Cook over medium heat, stirring occasionally, until golden, 7–10 minutes. Add the fennel and carrots; cook, stirring occasionally, 1–2 minutes.

3. Add the broth, wine, tomatoes, bay leaves, salt, and pepper; bring to a boil, stirring constantly to scrape the browned bits from the bottom of the pan. Return the veal to the Dutch oven. Reduce the heat and simmer, covered, until the veal is very tender, about 1½ hours.

4. Combine the flour and water in a small bowl until smooth; stir in about ½ cup of the hot liquid from the Dutch oven until blended. Add the flour mixture and the rosemary to the Dutch oven and cook, stirring constantly, until the mixture simmers and thickens, about 3 minutes.

5. To make the gremolata, mince the remaining garlic clove. Combine the parsley, lemon rind, and garlic in a small bowl; set aside. Remove the bay leaves from the Osso Buco and serve with the gremolata.

Per serving (1 veal shank with ¼ of sauce and gremolata): 393 Cal, 10 g Fat, 2 g Sat Fat, 201 mg Chol, 504 mg Sod, 20 g Carb, 4 g Fib, 55 g Prot, 117 mg Calc. **POINTS: 8.**

Chicken Piccata

MAKES 4 SERVINGS

Lemon juice and mustard add a perky flavor to this variation on veal piccata. To lightly pound the chicken, place each breast between 2 sheets of wax paper and pound to between ¼- and ½-inch thick with a mallet or rolling pin.

2 tablespoons coarse-grained Dijon mustard
1 large egg
½ cup Italian-seasoned dried bread crumbs
4 (¼-pound) skinless boneless chicken breast halves, lightly pounded
2 teaspoons olive oil
2 tablespoons dry vermouth or chicken broth
1 tablespoon fresh lemon juice
1 tablespoon minced fresh parsley
Lemon slices

1. Combine the mustard and egg in a shallow bowl. Place the bread crumbs on a sheet of wax paper. Dip the chicken in the mustard mixture, then in the bread crumbs.

2. Heat a large nonstick skillet over medium heat. Swirl in the oil, then add the chicken. Cook, until golden and cooked through, about 5 minutes on each side. Transfer the chicken to a platter and keep warm.

3. Add the vermouth and lemon juice to the same skillet. Simmer 30 seconds; stir in the parsley. Pour the sauce over the chicken and garnish with the lemon slices.

Per serving (1 chicken cutlet with ¼ of sauce): 225 Cal, 7 g Fat, 2 g Sat Fat, 116 mg Chol, 368 mg Sod, 11 g Carb, 0 g Fib, 26 g Prot, 50 mg Calc. *POINTS: 5.*

now, that's italian!

Chicken Saltimbocca

MAKES 6 SERVINGS

Saltimbocca is traditionally made with veal cutlets and can be rolled (as we've done here) or left flat. Guests and family alike will love our version, done with chicken cutlets that have been stuffed with flavorful prosciutto and sharp provolone, then bathed in a delicious Marsala sauce. Serve it with bow-tie pasta.

6 (¼-pound) chicken cutlets
1 tablespoon minced fresh sage leaves, or 1 teaspoon dried
¼ teaspoon salt
6 thin slices prosciutto (about 2 ounces)
¼ pound sharp provolone cheese, cut into 6 thin slices
1 tablespoon olive oil
1 teaspoon butter
1 onion, finely chopped
⅓ cup Marsala

1. Lightly pound the cutlets between 2 sheets of wax paper with a mallet or rolling pin until thin but not torn. Sprinkle with the sage and salt. Top with the prosciutto and cheese slices. Roll up the cutlets from short sides and secure with toothpicks. Refrigerate, covered, for 1 hour or overnight.
2. Heat a large nonstick skillet over medium-high heat. Swirl in the oil and butter, then add the chicken rolls. Cook until lightly browned, about 2 minutes on each side. Transfer the rolls to a plate. Add the onion to the same skillet and cook, stirring occasionally, until golden, 7–10 minutes. Add the Marsala and the browned chicken rolls to the skillet; bring to a boil. Reduce the heat and simmer, covered, until just cooked through, about 8 minutes.

Per serving (1 chicken roll with 2 tablespoons sauce): 249 Cal, 12 g Fat, 5 g Sat Fat, 84 mg Chol, 578 mg Sod, 3 g Carb, 0 g Fib, 30 g Prot, 154 mg Calc. **POINTS: 6.**

clever cook's tip

Refrigerate leftovers, covered, for up to 2 days. To reheat, microwave one chicken roll in a covered microwaveproof dish on High until heated through, about 3 minutes.

Chicken Saltimbocca

Sausage and Broccoli Rabe Risotto

MAKES 6 SERVINGS

A classic combination, sausage and broccoli rabe provide a welcome contrast of flavors and textures for this creamy risotto. For perfect risotto every time, use a short-grain rice, preferably Arborio.

3 cups low-sodium chicken broth
1 tablespoon olive oil
1 onion, finely chopped
1¼ cups Arborio or short-grain white rice
⅓ cup dry white wine
¼ teaspoon freshly ground pepper
¼ cup chopped fresh flat-leaf parsley
½ pound hot Italian turkey sausage, casings removed and crumbled
½ bunch broccoli rabe, rinsed and chopped

1. To make the risotto, bring the broth to a boil in a medium saucepan. Reduce the heat and keep at a simmer.

2. Heat a large nonstick saucepan over medium heat. Swirl in the oil, then add the onion. Cook, stirring occasionally, until softened, 3–5 minutes. Add the rice and cook until the outer shell is lightly toasted, 2–3 minutes.

3. Add the wine, pepper, and ½ cup of the broth and stir until the liquid is absorbed. Continue to add the broth, ½ cup at a time, stirring until it is absorbed before adding more, until the rice is just tender and the mixture is creamy. The cooking time from the first addition of broth should be 20–24 minutes.

4. Meanwhile, spray a nonstick skillet with nonstick spray and set over medium heat. Add the sausage and cook, stirring occasionally, until lightly browned, about 5 minutes. Add the broccoli rabe; cover and cook until wilted and softened, about 7 minutes. With a fork, stir the sausage and broccoli rabe into the risotto.

Per serving (1 cup): 291 Cal, 7 g Fat, 2 g Sat Fat, 22 mg Chol, 360 mg Sod, 43 g Carb, 1 g Fib, 13 g Prot, 43 mg Calc. **POINTS: 6.**

clever cook's tip

Timing and temperature are key to successful risotto making. Be sure to keep the cooking broth just at a simmer on a nearby burner. Start counting total risotto cooking time from the first addition of broth. Cook the risotto over medium to medium-low heat, or just enough heat to maintain a gentle simmer with each addition of liquid. Check the rice after 18–20 minutes cooking time. It should be tender and need just another couple of minutes at most.

Hearty Turkey Ragù

MAKES 6 SERVINGS ☕

Ragù is a thick, full-bodied meat sauce from Bologna that simmers for a long time. Here we use ground turkey, eggplant, and mushrooms, which require little time to cook, making this recipe an easy weeknight dish. Serve with grilled polenta slices, a favorite risotto, or cooked brown rice.

- **2 teaspoons olive oil**
- **1 onion, finely chopped**
- **1 green bell pepper, seeded and chopped**
- **2 garlic cloves, minced**
- **1 pound ground skinless turkey breast**
- **1 (28-ounce) can crushed tomatoes**
- **1 (1-pound) eggplant, unpeeled and cut into ½-inch chunks**
- **½ pound white mushrooms, halved**
- **¾ teaspoon salt**
- **½ teaspoon coarsely ground black pepper**
- **2 tablespoons chopped fresh oregano, or 2 teaspoons dried**

1. Heat a large nonstick Dutch oven over medium-high heat. Swirl in the oil, then add the onion, bell pepper, and garlic. Cook, stirring occasionally, until softened, about 8 minutes. Add the turkey and cook, breaking up the turkey with a wooden spoon, until the liquid evaporates and the turkey begins to brown, about 6 minutes.

2. Add the tomatoes, eggplant, mushrooms, salt, and pepper; bring to a boil. Reduce the heat and simmer, uncovered, stirring occasionally, 20 minutes. Stir in the oregano and simmer until the eggplant is softened and the flavors are developed, about 10 minutes longer.

Per serving (1⅓ cups): 191 Cal, 3 g Fat, 0 g Sat Fat, 55 mg Chol, 505 mg Sod, 20 g Carb, 6 g Fib, 24 g Prot, 69 mg Calc. **POINTS: 3.**

clever cook's tip

To protect your nonstick cookware, invest in a wooden spoon or long-handled nonstick fork to use when breaking up and browning clumps of ground meat.

Lasagna with Meat Sauce

MAKES 8 SERVINGS

Fennel-flavored sweet Italian sausage, with all its calories and **POINTS**, is often used in making lasagna. To cut the fat, we've substituted fennel seeds, toasted to bring out their flavor, and lean ground beef. Pecorino Romano, a sharp, aged sheep's-milk cheese, adds just the right bite to this dish. Serve with a spinach and mushroom salad.

9 lasagna noodles
1 teaspoon fennel seeds
1 teaspoon olive oil
½ pound lean ground beef (10% or less fat)
1 onion, chopped
1 red bell pepper, seeded and chopped
1 zucchini, chopped
2 (15-ounce) containers refrigerated marinara sauce
1½ cups nonfat ricotta cheese
½ cup shredded part-skim mozzarella cheese
¼ cup grated Pecorino Romano cheese

1. Cook the lasagna noodles according to package directions. Drain and rinse the noodles, then set aside.

2. To toast and grind the fennel seeds, place them in a small dry skillet over medium-low heat. Cook, shaking the pan and stirring constantly, until lightly browned and fragrant, 2–3 minutes. (Watch them carefully when toasting; seeds can burn quickly.) Transfer the seeds to a coffee grinder and grind to a powder. Or pound the seeds between two clean kitchen towels with a mallet until finely crushed.

3. Heat a large nonstick skillet over medium-high heat. Swirl in the oil, then add the beef, onion, bell pepper, and zucchini. Cook, stirring occasionally, until all the pan juices evaporate and the beef browns, about 10 minutes. Stir in the marinara sauce and fennel; bring to a boil. Reduce the heat and simmer, uncovered, until slightly thickened and the flavors blend, about 10 minutes.

4. Preheat the oven to 375° F. Spread one-fourth of the meat sauce in a 9 x 13-inch baking dish. Top with 3 of the noodles; spread with ½ cup of the ricotta. Repeat the layering twice, ending with the meat sauce.

5. Cover with foil and bake 30 minutes. Remove the foil and sprinkle with the mozzarella and Romano. Bake until heated through and the cheeses are lightly browned, about 20 minutes longer. Let stand 10 minutes before serving.

Per serving (⅛ of lasagna): 295 Cal, 9 g Fat, 3 g Sat Fat, 20 mg Chol, 589 mg Sod, 33 g Carb, 5 g Fib, 21 g Prot, 355 mg Calc. **POINTS: 6.**

clever cook's tip

To make ahead, assemble the lasagna without the cheeses; cover and refrigerate up to 2 days, or freeze up to 2 months. To reheat, thaw (if frozen) overnight in the refrigerator, cover with foil, and bake 45 minutes. Uncover, add the cheeses, and bake until heated through.

Spaghetti and Meatballs

MAKES 10 SERVINGS

A terrific weeknight standby, the meatballs and sauce can be made ahead and kept in the refrigerator for up to 2 days or in the freezer for up to 3 months.

1 tablespoon olive oil

2 onions, finely chopped

4 garlic cloves, minced

1 pound ground skinless turkey breast

½ pound lean ground pork (10% or less fat)

½ cup Italian-seasoned dried bread crumbs

¼ cup grated Parmesan cheese

1 large egg

2 egg whites

¼ cup fat-free milk

2 teaspoons Worcestershire sauce

¾ teaspoon salt

¼ teaspoon freshly ground pepper

1 (28-ounce) can crushed tomatoes

2 tablespoons chopped fresh oregano leaves, or 2 teaspoons dried

¾ pound spaghetti

1 ounce Parmesan cheese, shaved

1. Preheat the oven to 350° F. Spray a 10 x 15-inch jelly-roll pan with nonstick spray; set aside.

2. Heat a large nonstick skillet over medium-high heat. Swirl in the oil, then add the onions and garlic. Cook, stirring occasionally, until golden, 7–10 minutes.

3. Combine the turkey, pork, bread crumbs, grated Parmesan, egg, egg whites, milk, Worcestershire sauce, salt, pepper, and half of the cooked onions and garlic in a large bowl. Shape into 20 balls and place in a single layer without touching each other on the jelly-roll pan. Bake until lightly browned, about 20 minutes.

4. Bring the tomatoes and the remaining half of the cooked onions and garlic to a boil in a large saucepan; add the meatballs. Reduce the heat and simmer, covered, until the meatballs are cooked through, 18–20 minutes. Stir in the oregano.

5. Meanwhile cook the spaghetti according to package directions; drain. Toss the spaghetti with the meatballs in a large serving bowl and serve with the shaved Parmesan.

Per serving (2 meatballs with a generous ¾ cup spaghetti and sauce): 319 Cal, 5 g Fat, 2 g Sat Fat, 72 mg Chol, 602 mg Sod, 41 g Carb, 4 g Fib, 27 g Prot, 143 mg Calc. *POINTS: 6.*

Linguine Carbonara

Pancetta, an Italian bacon cured in salt and seasonings, is so flavorful that only a little is needed. To better appreciate its great taste, we sprinkle it on at the end. You can find it in the deli section of large supermarkets.

½ **pound linguine**
1 **ounce thinly sliced pancetta, chopped**
2 **teaspoons olive oil**
1 **onion, chopped**
¾ **cup fat-free egg substitute**
¼ **cup nonfat sour cream**
¼ **cup grated Parmesan cheese**
½ **teaspoon coarsely ground black pepper**

1. Cook the linguine according to package directions; drain, reserving 2 tablespoons of the cooking liquid. Return linguine and reserved liquid to the cooking pot; cover and keep warm.

2. Meanwhile, cook the pancetta in a medium nonstick skillet over medium-high heat until crisp. Transfer the pancetta to a plate and set aside. Heat the oil in the same skillet, then add the onion. Cook, stirring occasionally, until golden, 7–10 minutes.

3. Combine the egg substitute, sour cream, Parmesan, and pepper in a small bowl. Add the cooked onion and the egg mixture to the linguine. Cook over low heat just until heated through, about 1 minute. (Do not boil or the egg will overcook.) Serve sprinkled with the cooked pancetta.

Per serving (generous 1 cup): 340 Cal, 6 g Fat, 2 g Sat Fat, 7 mg Chol, 263 mg Sod, 52 g Carb, 3 g Fib, 17 g Prot, 141 mg Calc. **POINTS: 7.**

clever cook's tip

For a more tasty variation, and an additional ½ **POINT** per serving, add 2 cups frozen peas to the linguine during the last minute of cooking.

Fresh Fettuccine with Homemade Pesto

MAKES 4 SERVINGS ⏲

Use summer's bounty of fresh basil by doubling the pesto recipe (without the cheese) and freezing half for up to 6 months. This recipe is delicious served with a large tossed leafy green salad and crusty whole-wheat Italian bread.

1½ cups lightly packed fresh basil leaves

2 tablespoons pine nuts, toasted

2 tablespoons low-sodium chicken or vegetable broth

2 teaspoons extra-virgin olive oil

1 garlic clove, sliced

¼ teaspoon salt

1 (9-ounce) package fresh fettuccine

3 tablespoons shredded Parmesan cheese

Freshly ground pepper, to taste

1. To prepare the pesto, puree the basil, pine nuts, broth, oil, garlic, and salt in a blender or food processor until a smooth paste is formed.

2. Meanwhile, cook the fettuccine according to package directions, drain, reserving 2 tablespoons of the cooking liquid. Transfer the fettuccine and reserved liquid to a serving bowl and keep warm. Add the pesto and Parmesan; toss to coat. Serve with the pepper.

Per serving (generous 1 cup): 256 Cal, 7 g Fat, 2 g Sat Fat, 50 mg Chol, 254 mg Sod, 37 g Carb, 3 g Fib, 11 g Prot, 102 mg Calc. *POINTS: 5.*

clever cook's tip

Toasting pine nuts brings out their flavor. To toast, place the pine nuts in a small nonstick skillet over medium-low heat, shaking the pan and stirring constantly until nuts are golden and fragrant, about 2 minutes.

now, that's italian!

Pasta Primavera

Here, a delicate broth-based sauce allows all the flavors of the fresh vegetables to shine. Substitute fettuccine for the penne, and Parmesan for the Asiago, if you prefer.

½ pound penne
1 tablespoon extra-virgin olive oil
1 onion, chopped
3 garlic cloves, minced
¾ cup low-sodium vegetable broth
4 carrots, cut diagonally into ½-inch-thick slices
1 pound broccoli crowns, cut into florets (about 4 cups)
1 zucchini, cut diagonally into ½-inch-thick slices
1 yellow squash, cut diagonally into ½-inch-thick slices
½ teaspoon salt
¼ teaspoon coarsely ground black pepper
¼ cup grated Asiago cheese
12 fresh basil leaves, thinly sliced

1. Cook the penne according to package directions; drain and deep warm.
2. Meanwhile, heat a 12- to 14-inch nonstick skillet over medium-high heat. Swirl in the oil, then add the onion and garlic. Cook, stirring frequently, until golden, about 5 minutes. Add the broth and carrots; bring to a boil. Reduce the heat and simmer, covered, 5 minutes.
3. Add the broccoli, zucchini, yellow squash, salt, and pepper; return to a boil. Reduce the heat and simmer, covered, until the vegetables are just crisp-tender, 6–7 minutes. Toss with the pasta. Serve at once sprinkled with the Asiago and basil.

Per serving (generous 2 cups): 338 Cal, 7 g Fat, 2 g Sat Fat, 6 mg Chol, 382 mg Sod, 58 g Carb, 9 g Fib, 13 g Prot, 166 mg Calc. **POINTS: 7.**

clever cook's tip

For a brightly colored primavera, it's important to cook the vegetables just until they are crisp-tender and still colorful. If you overcook the vegetables or let them sit too long, they will lose their vivid color and texture.

Neapolitan Cookies

MAKES 6 DOZEN

These fanciful cookies were handed down from an Italian mother who has been making them every Christmas for the past 50 years. They are rich and delicious so you only need one or two.

2 cups all-purpose flour

1 teaspoon baking soda

¼ teaspoon salt

1 (7- or 8-ounce) tube or can almond paste

1 cup butter, softened

1 cup sugar

4 large eggs

1 teaspoon vanilla extract

½ teaspoon almond extract

10 drops red food coloring

6 drops green food coloring

¼ cup seedless red raspberry jam

¼ cup apricot preserves

1 (6-ounce) package semisweet chocolate chips, melted

1. Preheat the oven to 350° F. Spray three 9 x 13-inch baking pans with nonstick spray. Line the pans with wax paper; lightly spray the paper with nonstick spray.

2. Combine the flour, baking soda, and salt in a medium bowl; set aside.

3. With an electric mixer on high speed, beat the almond paste, butter, and sugar until light and fluffy. Add the eggs, one at a time, beating well after each addition. Beat in the vanilla and almond extracts.

4. With the electric mixer on low speed, stir in the flour mixture until just blended. Divide dough into thirds (about 1½ cups each); transfer to three medium bowls. Tint one batch of dough pink with the red food coloring and another batch green with the green food coloring. Leave remaining dough untinted.

5. Scrape the untinted dough into a baking pan, the pink dough into another, and the green dough into the third; spreading each batch until smooth. Bake until the edges just begin to turn golden, about 12 minutes. Cool the layers in the pans on racks completely.

6. Invert the layers onto a work surface and remove the wax paper. Spread the raspberry jam over the green layer; top with the uncolored layer. Spread the apricot jam on the uncolored layer and top with the pink layer. Wrap in plastic wrap, place on a cutting board, and top with another cutting board or large heavy flat pan to weigh it down. Refrigerate overnight.

7. Remove the plastic wrap. Spread the melted chocolate over the top layer; let cool and set slightly. With a large sharp knife, cut lengthwise into twelve ¾-inch strips and then cut crosswise into six 2-inch strips, making a total of 72 cookies.

Per serving (1 cookie): 80 Cal, 4 g Fat, 2 g Sat Fat, 19 mg Chol, 31 mg Sod, 10 g Carb, 0 g Fib, 1 g Prot, 8 mg Calc. *POINTS: 2.*

Cannoli

MAKES 6 SERVINGS

A favorite Italian bakery item, cannoli are a cinch to make at home. The secret is to use a piping bag fitted with a large tip to pipe the sweetened ricotta mixture into the crisp pastry tubes. You can keep this luscious filling on hand in the refrigerator for up to two days.

1 cup fat-free ricotta
   cheese
2 tablespoons
   confectioners'
   sugar
2 tablespoons
   coarsely shredded
   fresh orange rind
1½ teaspoons orange
   liqueur or vanilla
   extract
2 tablespoons mini
   semisweet
   chocolate chips
6 prepared
   cannoli shells
Confectioners' sugar,
   for dusting

1. Combine the ricotta, sugar, orange rind, liqueur or extract, and chocolate chips in a medium bowl.

2. Spoon the mixture into a piping bag fitted with a large tip, and pipe the mixture—dividing it evenly—into the 6 shells. Dust with confectioners' sugar.

Per serving (1 cannoli): 149 Cal, 5 g Fat, 2 g Sat Fat, 5 mg Chol, 82 mg Sod, 16 g Carb, 1 g Fib, 8 g Prot, 205 mg Calc. ***POINTS: 3.***

clever cook's tip

To add a touch of elegance, serve the cannoli with frosted grapes. Wash small bunches of five or six grapes and while still wet, roll in sugar until evenly coated; allow to dry before using.

Neapolitan
Cookies and
Cannoli

7 totally thai

Coconut-Curry Pork Satay

MAKES 6 SERVINGS

These Asian-style kebabs are a must-have on every Thai menu. For this recipe, thin strips of pork are thread on skewers and served with a spicy peanut-based dipping sauce—but feel free to substitute chicken or beef. Satay is usually served as an appetizer (a terrific choice for parties), but it's also perfect for busy weeknights, served over rice with a side of steamed broccoli.

½ cup light coconut milk

2 tablespoons packed light brown sugar

1 tablespoon reduced-sodium soy sauce

1 tablespoon ketchup

1 tablespoon reduced-fat peanut butter

1 teaspoon Thai fish sauce (nam pla)

½ teaspoon crushed red pepper

2 tablespoons chopped fresh cilantro

1 pound boneless pork tenderloin, trimmed of all visible fat, cut diagonally into ¼-inch-thick slices

1 teaspoon Asian (dark) sesame oil

1 clove garlic, minced

½ teaspoon salt

½ teaspoon freshly ground pepper

8 green leaf lettuce leaves

1. Spray the grill or broiler rack with nonstick spray; prepare the grill or preheat the broiler.

2. To make the dipping sauce, bring the coconut milk, brown sugar, soy sauce, ketchup, peanut butter, fish sauce, and crushed red pepper to a boil in a medium saucepan. Cook, stirring occasionally, over medium-high heat until the flavors are blended and the mixture thickens slightly, about 5 minutes. Remove from the heat; stir in the cilantro. Cover and keep warm.

3. Combine the pork, sesame oil, garlic, salt, and pepper in a medium bowl; toss to coat.

4. Thread the pork onto each of 12 (6-inch) metal or bamboo skewers. Grill or broil the pork 5 inches from the heat until cooked through, about 2 minutes on each side. Transfer the skewers to a lettuce-lined platter; brush with some of the sauce. Serve the remaining sauce on the side.

Per serving (1 skewer with 2 tablespoons sauce): 157 Cal, 6 g Fat, 2 g Sat Fat, 45 mg Chol, 456 mg Sod, 7 g Carb, 0 g Fib, 17 g Prot, 11 mg Calc. *POINTS: 4.*

clever cook's tip

Satay typically uses bamboo skewers, which will stay cooler on the grill than the metal variety. If you opt for these, be sure to soak the skewers in cold water at least 1 hour before using, so they won't burn during grilling.

Velvet Corn Soup with Shrimp

MAKES 4 SERVINGS

This creamy corn soup can be made in a matter of minutes. You can substitute strips of cooked chicken breast for the shrimp, or for a special touch, add some canned crabmeat.

1 teaspoon canola oil

3 cloves garlic, minced

1 tablespoon minced peeled fresh ginger

½ teaspoon hot chili paste

4 cups reduced-sodium chicken broth

1 (14¾-ounce) can cream-style corn

1 (8-ounce) package frozen cooked salad shrimp, thawed

2 teaspoons Thai fish sauce (nam pla)

1 tablespoon water

2 teaspoons cornstarch

1 teaspoon sugar

1 teaspoon Asian (dark) sesame oil

1 large egg, lightly beaten

¼ cup chopped fresh cilantro

¼ teaspoon paprika

1. Heat a large nonstick saucepan over medium heat. Swirl in the oil, then add the garlic, ginger, and chili paste. Cook, stirring, until fragrant, 1 minute.

2. Stir in the broth, corn, shrimp, and fish sauce; bring to a boil. Simmer until the flavors are blended, 15 minutes.

3. Meanwhile, whisk the water, cornstarch, sugar, and sesame oil in a small bowl until blended; stir into the soup. Stir in the egg. Return the soup to a simmer and cook until the soup thickens slightly and the egg sets into long strands, about 3 minutes. Stir in the cilantro and the paprika. Serve at once.

Per serving (1½ cups): 201 Cal, 6 g Fat, 2 g Sat Fat, 138 mg Chol, 755 mg Sod, 24 g Carb, 2 g Fib, 16 g Prot, 49 mg Calc. **POINTS: 4.**

Vegetarian Spring Rolls

Vegetarian Spring Rolls

MAKES 8 SERVINGS

Vietnamese spring rolls aren't fried. Rather, they're mainly rice noodles with cabbage, shrimp, or pork enclosed in a translucent rice-paper wrapper. We've added carrots and onion to this vegetarian filling and serve the rolls with a light lime dipping sauce. If you choose to make the rolls ahead, just be sure to keep them covered with a damp towel, wrapped tightly in plastic wrap, so they won't dry out.

DIPPING SAUCE

¼ cup fresh lime juice
3 tablespoons sugar
2 tablespoons chopped cilantro
2 teaspoons Thai fish sauce (nam pla)
1 teaspoon minced peeled fresh ginger
1 clove garlic, minced
1 teaspoon Asian (dark) sesame oil
Pinch crushed red pepper

SPRING ROLLS

1 teaspoon canola oil
1 clove garlic, minced
1 teaspoon minced peeled fresh ginger
½ pound savoy cabbage, shredded
1 onion, sliced
1 tablespoon reduced-sodium soy sauce
2 ounces rice-stick noodles
½ cup grated carrot
2 teaspoons Asian (dark) sesame oil
16 (6-inch) round rice-paper wrappers

1. To make the dipping sauce, whisk the lime juice, sugar, cilantro, fish sauce, ginger, garlic, sesame oil, and crushed red pepper in a small bowl. Set aside.

2. To make the spring rolls, heat a large nonstick skillet over medium heat. Swirl in the canola oil, then add the garlic and ginger. Cook, stirring, until fragrant, 1 minute. Stir in the cabbage, onion, and soy sauce. Increase the heat to medium-high. Cook, stirring occasionally, until the vegetables are very tender, about 15 minutes. Transfer the cabbage mixture to a medium bowl.

3. Meanwhile, place the rice noodles in a large bowl and add enough hot water to cover; let stand until the noodles are soft, about 10 minutes. Drain, rinse with cold water, and drain again. Cut the noodles into 2-inch lengths; stir into the cabbage mixture. Add the carrot and sesame oil; toss to coat.

4. To assemble the rolls, dip one rice wrapper in a bowl of warm water and place it on a clean kitchen towel. Place about 2 tablespoons of the vegetable mixture in the center of the wrapper. Fold in the sides, then roll up to completely enclose the filling. Repeat with the remaining rice wrappers and vegetable mixture to make 16 rolls. Transfer the rolls to a cutting board and slice each in half. Serve with the dipping sauce.

Per serving (2 rolls with 1 tablespoon sauce): 171 Cal, 4 g Fat, 0 g Sat Fat, 0 mg Chol, 202 mg Sod, 32 g Carb, 2 g Fib, 3 g Prot, 21 mg Calc. **POINTS: 3.**

Cabbage Roll Soup

MAKES 4 SERVINGS

Our delectable stuffed rolls are simmered in a broth infused with fresh lemongrass and spicy fresh ginger. We use ground turkey breast in the filling, but chicken, lean ground beef, or pork would work just as nicely.

CABBAGE ROLLS

- 12 small savoy cabbage leaves, large ribs removed
- 1 pound ground skinless turkey breast
- 1 tablespoon minced peeled fresh ginger
- 1 clove garlic, minced
- 2 teaspoons Thai fish sauce (nam pla)
- 6 scallions, chopped
- 2 teaspoons Asian (dark) sesame oil

BROTH

- 1 teaspoon canola oil
- ¼ cup sliced scallions
- 2 cloves garlic, minced
- 2 teaspoons minced peeled fresh ginger
- 1 teaspoon finely chopped fresh lemongrass
- 4 cups reduced-sodium chicken broth
- 2 tablespoons fresh lime juice
- 1 tablespoon reduced-sodium soy sauce
- ¼ cup fresh cilantro leaves

1. To make the cabbage rolls, fill a large saucepan two-thirds full of water and bring to a boil. Add the cabbage leaves and boil until the leaves are wilted, about 30 seconds. Drain; set aside and cool.

2. Combine the turkey, ginger, garlic, fish sauce, scallions, and sesame oil in a large bowl until blended.

3. Working 1 cabbage leaf at a time, place 2 rounded tablespoons of the turkey mixture in the center of the bottom third of the leaf. Fold over the sides, then roll up from the bottom of the leaf to form a package. Secure the bottom of the package with a toothpick. Repeat with remaining leaves and turkey filling to make 12 cabbage rolls; set aside.

4. To make the broth, heat a large saucepan over medium-high heat. Swirl in the oil, then add the scallions, garlic, ginger, and lemongrass. Cook, stirring, until fragrant, about 1 minute. Add the broth, lime juice, and soy sauce; bring to a boil.

5. Add the cabbage rolls to the broth. Cover and simmer until the flavors are blended and the rolls are cooked through, about 30 minutes. Remove from the heat. Stir in the cilantro leaves. Serve at once.

Per serving (3 rolls with 1 cup broth): 220 Cal, 6 g Fat, 1 g Sat Fat, 86 mg Chol, 552 mg Sod, 7 g Carb, 2 g Fib, 35 g Prot, 67 mg Calc. **POINTS: 5.**

clever cook's tip

Fresh lemongrass has long thin leaves on a woody base. It can be refrigerated, tightly wrapped, for up to 2 weeks. Dried lemongrass is now available in the spice aisle of many supermarkets. You can use ¼ teaspoon dried lemongrass or 1 teaspoon grated lemon rind as a substitute.

Thai Noodles with Chicken and Vegetables

Noodles are a staple ingredient of Thai cuisine. Most recipes call for rice noodles, but Thai cooks also use flat Chinese egg noodles, as well as bean-thread (cellophane) noodles. "No-cook" rice-stick noodles are our choice for this zesty dish. They couldn't be easier to prepare—just soften in hot water for a few minutes, then drain. Capellini (or angel-hair pasta) is a good substitute, but you'll have to cook it according to package directions.

¼ **pound rice-stick noodles**

1 **teaspoon canola oil**

1 **pound skinless boneless chicken breasts**

2 **cloves garlic, minced**

1 **teaspoon minced peeled fresh ginger**

1 **teaspoon hot chili paste**

½ **cup reduced-sodium chicken broth**

¼ **cup fresh lime juice**

2 **tablespoons packed light brown sugar**

½ **teaspoon Thai fish sauce (nam pla)**

1 **cup fresh snow peas, trimmed**

3 **scallions, thinly sliced**

1 **carrot, cut into matchstick-thin strips**

¼ **cup chopped fresh cilantro**

1. Place the noodles in a large bowl and add enough hot water to cover; let stand until the noodles are soft, about 10 minutes. Drain, transfer the noodles to a large bowl of cold water to cool, and drain again. Set aside.

2. Meanwhile, heat a large nonstick skillet over medium-high heat. Swirl in the oil, then add the chicken. Cook until the chicken is browned, 8 minutes. Transfer the chicken to a cutting board; let stand 5 minutes. Slice chicken into ¼-inch-thick slices; set aside.

3. Heat the same skillet over low heat. Add the garlic, ginger, and chili paste. Cook, stirring, until fragrant, about 1 minute. Add the broth, lime juice, brown sugar, and fish sauce; cook, stirring, until the sugar dissolves, about 30 seconds.

4. Add the snow peas, scallions, and carrots; cook 1 minute. Stir in the chicken and the drained noodles; cook, tossing gently, until mixed and heated through, 2–3 minutes longer. Stir in the cilantro. Serve at once.

Per serving (1 cup): 201 Cal, 3 g Fat, 1 g Sat Fat, 42 mg Chol, 100 mg Sod, 25 g Carb, 2 g Fib, 18 g Prot, 44 mg Calc. *POINTS: 4.*

Shrimp Pad Thai

This classic noodle dish is a perennial Thai favorite. Consisting of shrimp and crunchy bean sprouts, it's bathed in a sweet-and-sour sauce, then sprinkled with chopped roasted peanuts. Slivered pieces of chicken or lean pork can be substituted for the shrimp, or for a vegetarian version, use strips of extra-firm tofu.

¼ **pound rice-stick noodles**

1 **teaspoon canola oil**

½ **pound large shrimp, peeled and deveined**

4 **scallions, chopped**

2 **cloves garlic, minced**

2 **egg whites, lightly beaten**

2 **tablespoons Thai fish sauce (nam pla)**

2 **tablespoons sugar**

1 **tablespoon hot chili sauce**

1 **tablespoon reduced-sodium soy sauce**

2 **cups bean sprouts**

3 **tablespoons dry-roasted peanuts, chopped**

¼ **cup fresh cilantro leaves**

1. Place the noodles in a large bowl and add enough hot water to cover; let stand until the noodles are soft, about 10 minutes. Drain, transfer the noodles to a large bowl of cold water to cool, and drain again. Set aside.

2. Heat a large nonstick skillet over medium-high heat. Swirl in the oil, then add the shrimp. Cook until the shrimp are just opaque in the center, about 3 minutes. Add the scallions and garlic. Cook until fragrant, about 10 seconds. Add the egg whites, stirring gently, until they begin to set, about 30 seconds. Add the fish sauce, sugar, chili sauce, and soy sauce; cook, stirring, until the sugar dissolves, about 30 seconds. Add the drained noodles and the bean sprouts; cook, tossing gently, until mixed and heated through, 2–3 minutes longer. Sprinkle with the peanuts and cilantro.

Per serving (1 cup): 243 Cal, 4 g Fat, 1 g Sat Fat, 67 mg Chol, 1,001 mg Sod, 36 g Carb, 3 g Fib, 15 g Prot, 56 mg Calc. **POINTS: 5.**

Shrimp Pad Thai

Grilled Chicken and Jasmine Rice Salad

MAKES 6 SERVINGS

Jasmine rice is an aromatic grain traditionally grown in Thailand and has a flavor and fragrance similar to basmati rice. Today, it's also harvested on our shores. Served with grilled chicken, tender baby spinach, and vegetables with a refreshing mint dressing, it makes an exceptionally delicious main-dish salad.

2 cups water
1 cup jasmine or long-grain white rice
¼ cup fresh lime juice
2 tablespoons seasoned rice vinegar
2 tablespoons chopped fresh mint
1 tablespoon Asian (dark) sesame oil
2 teaspoons sugar
¼ teaspoon crushed red pepper
1 (¼ pound) skinless boneless chicken breast
2 cups baby spinach, cleaned and chopped
1 cup bean sprouts
¼ cup chopped scallions

1. To make the rice, bring water to a boil in a medium saucepan; add the rice. Reduce the heat to low and simmer, covered, until the liquid is absorbed and the rice is tender, 20 minutes. Remove the saucepan from the heat and let the rice stand undisturbed 5 minutes. Fluff with a fork. Transfer the rice to a large bowl; cool completely.

2. To make the dressing, whisk the lime juice, vinegar, mint, sesame oil, sugar, and crushed red pepper in a small bowl until blended; set aside.

3. Spray the grill or broiler rack with nonstick spray; prepare the grill or preheat the broiler.

4. Grill or broil the chicken 5 inches from the heat, turning occasionally, until cooked through, 8–10 minutes. Transfer the chicken to a cutting board; cool and cut on the diagonal into thin slices.

5. Toss the rice with the spinach, bean sprouts, scallions, and half of the dressing. Divide the rice salad among six plates; top with the chicken. Drizzle the chicken with the remaining half of the dressing. Serve at once.

Per serving (1 cup): 173 Cal, 3 g Fat, 1 g Sat Fat, 10 mg Chol, 26 mg Sod, 30 g Carb, 1 g Fib, 7 g Prot, 30 mg Calc. **POINTS: 4.**

clever cook's tip

For a nutritional boost, substitute the jasmine rice with brown aromatic rice. It has a natural aroma and flavor similar to that of roasted nuts.

Roasted Chicken with Coconut-Lime Glaze

MAKES 6 SERVINGS

Once you try this Thai-style roast chicken, you may never go back to that plain old bird again! Its secret? Coconut milk, which is made by mixing grated fresh coconut meat with warm water and then squeezing out the rich, creamy juice. Light coconut milk is made from the second pressing, so it's far lower in fat and calories. (Don't confuse canned coconut milk with "cream of coconut," which is sweetened.)

- 2 tablespoons minced onion
- 1 tablespoon minced peeled fresh ginger
- 1 tablespoon finely chopped fresh lemongrass, or 1 teaspoon dried
- 1 (3½ pound) roasting chicken
- 1 cup light coconut milk
- 2 tablespoons fresh lime juice
- 1 tablespoon chicken broth
- 1 tablespoon light brown sugar
- 1 teaspoon reduced-sodium soy sauce
- ½ teaspoon Thai fish sauce (nam pla)
- ½ teaspoon Asian (dark) sesame oil
- 2 tablespoons chopped fresh basil

1. Preheat the oven to 400° F. Spray the rack of a roasting pan with nonstick spray and place in the pan.
2. Combine the onion, ginger, and lemongrass in a small bowl.
3. Gently loosen the skin from the breast and leg portions of the chicken; stuff the onion mixture evenly under the skin.
4. Pat the chicken dry with paper towels. Tuck the wings back and tie the legs together with kitchen twine. Place the chicken, breast-side up, in the roasting pan. Roast until an instant-read thermometer inserted in the inner thigh registers 180° F, about 1 hour and 15 minutes. Remove from the oven and let stand 10 minutes. Remove and discard the skin.
5. To make the glaze, combine the coconut milk, lime juice, broth, sugar, soy sauce, fish sauce, and sesame oil in a small saucepan; bring to a boil. Cook, stirring, over medium-high heat until the mixture reduces by half, about 10 minutes. Remove from the heat and stir in the basil.
6. Carve the chicken; spoon the warm glaze over the top. Serve at once.

Per serving (⅙ of chicken with 1 generous tablespoon glaze): 239 Cal, 11 g Fat, 4 g Sat Fat, 84 mg Chol, 174 mg Sod, 4 g Carb, 0 g Fib, 28 g Prot, 17 mg Calc. **POINTS: 6.**

clever cook's tip

To prepare fresh lemongrass, strip off and discard the outer fibrous leaves of the stalk, then finely chop (the tender part has the best flavor). You'll need about a 3-inch piece of lemongrass for this recipe.

Fiery Beef with Scallions and Cashews

MAKES 4 SERVINGS 🔥

Now you can enjoy steak Thai-barbecue style! We use lean, flavorful flank steak, marinated in a zesty blend of jalapeño, lemongrass, ginger, and hot pepper sauce. To keep the flank steak moist and tender, slice the steak thinly across the grain, then sear it quickly on the grill.

¼ cup honey

¼ cup minced onion

1 tablespoon minced peeled fresh ginger

1 tablespoon finely chopped fresh lemongrass, or 1 teaspoon dried

2 cloves garlic, finely chopped

1 jalapeño pepper, minced (wear gloves to prevent irritation)

1 tablespoon reduced-sodium soy sauce

1 teaspoon Thai fish sauce (nam pla)

1 teaspoon Asian (dark) sesame oil

2 or 3 drops hot pepper sauce

1 (1 pound) flank steak, trimmed of all visible fat, cut diagonally across the grain into ¼-inch-thick slices

¼ cup chopped scallions

3 tablespoons chopped cashews

1. To make the marinade, combine the honey, onion, ginger, lemongrass, garlic, jalapeño, soy sauce, fish sauce, sesame oil, and hot sauce in a large zip-close plastic bag; mix well. Add the steak, seal the bag, and turn several times to coat. Refrigerate the steak, turning the bag occasionally, at least 1 hour or overnight.

2. Spray the grill or broiler rack with nonstick spray; prepare the grill or preheat the broiler.

3. Remove the steak from the marinade, scraping off any excess. Discard the marinade. Thread the steak onto each of 8 (8-inch) metal skewers. Grill or broil the steak 5 inches from the heat until browned, 3 minutes on each side. Sprinkle the steak with the scallions and cashews.

Per serving (2 skewers): 240 Cal, 12 g Fat, 4 g Sat Fat, 59 mg Chol, 179 mg Sod, 8 g Carb, 0 g Fib, 25 g Prot, 15 mg Calc. *POINTS: 6.*

Spicy Lamb with Basil Jasmine Rice

MAKES 4 SERVINGS 🔥

You don't see lamb often on Thai menus, but these soy-and-honey-glazed kebabs are absolutely delicious. Another appealing factor of this recipe: The lamb needs to marinate only 30 minutes! A lovely side dish of jasmine rice tossed with lemon rind and chopped fresh basil rounds out the meal.

¼ cup finely chopped
   scallions
2 tablespoons honey
2 tablespoons
   reduced-sodium
   soy sauce
2 cloves garlic,
   minced
1 jalapeño pepper,
   minced (wear
   gloves to prevent
   irritation)
2 teaspoons minced
   peeled fresh ginger
1 pound boneless leg
   of lamb, trimmed
   of all visible fat, cut
   into 1-inch cubes
2 cups water
1 cup jasmine or
   long-grain
   white rice
½ teaspoon salt
3 tablespoons
   chopped fresh basil
1 tablespoon grated
   lemon rind

1. To make the marinade, combine the scallions, honey, soy sauce, garlic, jalapeño, and ginger in a large zip-close plastic bag; mix well. Add the lamb, seal the bag, and turn several times to coat. Refrigerate the lamb, turning the bag occasionally, 30 minutes.

2. To make the rice, bring the water to a boil in a medium saucepan; add the rice and the salt. Reduce the heat to low and simmer, covered, until the liquid is absorbed and the rice is tender, 20 minutes. Remove the saucepan from the heat, and let the rice stand undisturbed 10 minutes. Fluff with a fork; stir in the basil and lemon rind.

3. Meanwhile, spray the grill or broiler rack with nonstick spray; prepare the grill or preheat the broiler.

4. Remove the lamb from the marinade, scraping off any excess. Discard the marinade. Thread the lamb on each of 4 (12-inch) metal skewers. Grill or broil the lamb 5 inches from the heat, 3 minutes on each side for medium-rare. Serve with the rice.

Per serving (1 skewer with ¾ cup rice): 338 Cal, 6 g Fat, 2 g Sat Fat, 73 mg Chol, 423 mg Sod, 41 g Carb, 1 g Fib, 26 g Prot, 14 mg Calc.
POINTS: 7.

take-out tonight! **175**

Roasted Sesame Pork

Thai cooks are fond of combining sweet and sour flavors with meat. In this speedy weeknight roast, the soy and fish sauces balance out the sweetness of the honey, and the sesame seed coating adds a nutty flavor and crunchy texture to the pork.

1 tablespoon reduced-sodium soy sauce
1 tablespoon honey
1 teaspoon Asian (dark) sesame oil
1 teaspoon minced peeled fresh ginger
1 clove garlic, minced
1 (1-pound) pork tenderloin, trimmed of all visible fat
1 tablespoon sesame seeds

1. Preheat the oven to 425° F. Spray a shallow roasting pan with nonstick spray.
2. Combine the soy sauce, honey, sesame oil, ginger, and garlic in a large bowl. Pat the pork dry with paper towels; add it to the soy mixture and turn to evenly coat.
3. Place the pork in the roasting pan; press in the sesame seeds. Roast until an instant-read thermometer inserted into the thickest part of the pork registers 160° F, 20–25 minutes. Transfer the pork to a carving board and let stand 10 minutes before slicing.

Per serving (¼ of pork): 181 Cal, 6 g Fat, 2 g Sat Fat, 67 mg Chol, 200 mg Sod, 6 g Carb, 0 g Fib, 25 g Prot, 10 mg Calc. *POINTS: 4.*

clever cook's tip

For an extra protein boost, add any leftover pork to our Vegetarian Spring Rolls [page 167].

Spicy Thai Seafood Pot

MAKES 8 SERVINGS

A true seafood lover's delight, this luxurious stew is perfect company fare. Thai curry paste (a blend of chiles, garlic, onion, lemongrass, spices, and shrimp paste—available in Asian groceries) gives the dish its fiery flavor. Coconut milk, ginger, and chopped fresh basil lend a touch of sweetness.

- 1 teaspoon canola oil
- 2 cloves garlic, minced
- 1 tablespoon minced peeled fresh ginger
- 1 tablespoon packed light brown sugar
- 1 teaspoon Thai fish sauce (nam pla)
- ½ teaspoon Thai red curry paste
- 1 (14-ounce) can light coconut milk
- 1 dozen littleneck clams, cleaned and scrubbed
- 1 (2-pound) bag medium mussels, scrubbed and debearded
- ½ pound medium shrimp, peeled and deveined
- ½ cup chopped fresh basil

1. Heat a large nonstick saucepan over low heat. Swirl in the oil, then add the garlic, ginger, sugar, fish sauce, and curry paste. Cook, stirring constantly, until fragrant, 1 minute.

2. Stir in the coconut milk and the clams; increase the heat to medium and bring to a simmer. Cover and cook until the clams begin to open, about 5 minutes. Stir in the mussels and the shrimp. Cover and cook until the mussels have opened and the shrimp are pink, about 4 minutes. Stir in the basil. Serve at once.

Per serving (2 cups): 140 Cal, 7 g Fat, 3 g Sat Fat, 56 mg Chol, 288 mg Sod, 5 g Carb, 0 g Fib, 13 g Prot, 36 mg Calc. **POINTS: 3.**

clever cook's tip

When cooking with clams and mussels, it's important to check for freshness. Any shells that are open before cooking should be discarded, as well as any that do not open after cooking. (Before discarding a mussel that is open before cooking, tap on it gently. If it closes, then it's fine to use.)

Gingery Scallops and Vegetables

MAKES 4 SERVINGS

Scallops are delicate and take only minutes to cook, which is definitely an advantage if you're looking for flash-in-the-pan (everything's ready in less than twenty minutes!) dinner fare with a touch of elegance. For best results, pat the scallops dry with paper towels and sauté them in one layer in a hot pan. This will give the scallops a nice sear on the outside while remaining succulent and juicy inside.

2 teaspoons canola oil

1 pound sea scallops, muscle removed

1 tablespoon minced peeled fresh ginger

2 cloves garlic, minced

2 cups bean sprouts

1 cup fresh snow peas, trimmed and sliced diagonally in half

1 cup thinly sliced red bell pepper

½ cup shredded carrots

2 tablespoons light coconut milk

1 tablespoon packed light brown sugar

1 tablespoon reduced-sodium soy sauce

1. Heat in a large nonstick skillet over medium-high heat. Swirl in 1 teaspoon of the oil, then add the scallops. Cook, turning once, until golden brown on the outside and just opaque in the center, about 1 minute on each side. Transfer the scallops to a plate, cover, and keep warm.

2. Return the skillet to the heat. Swirl the remaining 1 teaspoon oil, then add the ginger and garlic. Cook, stirring, until fragrant, about 30 seconds. Add the bean sprouts, snow peas, bell pepper, and carrots; cook until the vegetables are tender-crisp, 2–3 minutes. Stir in the coconut milk, sugar, and soy sauce; cook until the sugar dissolves, 30 seconds. Return the scallops to the pan and toss to combine. Serve at once.

Per serving (1 cup): 148 Cal, 5 g Fat, 1 g Sat Fat, 18 mg Chol, 269 mg Sod, 14 g Carb, 3 g Fib, 13 g Prot, 47 mg Calc. **POINTS: 3.**

clever cook's tip

To save time, buy packaged preshredded carrots. You can also substitute shelled and deveined large shrimp for the scallops, just increase the cooking time to 1½ minutes on each side in Step 1.

Seared Salmon with Pickled Ginger and Garlic Sauce

MAKES 4 SERVINGS

Pickled ginger, fresh ginger preserved in seasoned vinegar, is often served as a condiment with Asian dishes. Its sweet, pungent taste complements spicy foods—like this grilled salmon served with garlicky vegetables.

- ½ cup chicken broth
- 1 tablespoon reduced-sodium soy sauce
- 1 tablespoon pickled ginger juice
- 1 teaspoon Asian (dark) sesame oil
- ½ teaspoon hot chili paste
- 1 teaspoon cornstarch
- 1 teaspoon canola oil
- 3 tablespoons chopped shallots
- 2 tablespoons pickled ginger, drained and chopped
- 2 cloves garlic, minced
- ½ pound asparagus, cut diagonally into 2-inch pieces
- 1 red bell pepper, seeded and cut into 1-inch chunks
- 1 tablespoon dried lemongrass
- 1 tablespoon packed light brown sugar
- 1 (1-pound) salmon fillet, cut into 4 equal pieces

1. Whisk the broth, soy sauce, ginger juice, sesame oil, chili paste, and cornstarch in a small bowl until blended; set aside.

2. Heat a large nonstick skillet over low heat. Swirl in the oil, then add the shallots, pickled ginger, and garlic. Cook, stirring, until fragrant, about 30 seconds. Add the asparagus and bell pepper. Increase the heat to medium-high; cook until the vegetables are tender-crisp, 5 minutes. Stir in the broth mixture; bring to a boil. Cook, stirring, until the mixture thickens slightly.

3. Meanwhile, combine the lemongrass and brown sugar in a small bowl; rub over both sides of the salmon pieces.

4. Spray the grill with nonstick spray and prepare the grill or spray a nonstick ridged grill pan with nonstick spray and set over high heat. Grill the salmon 5 inches from heat until opaque in the center, 4 minutes on each side.

5. Divide the vegetable mixture among four plates; top with the salmon.

Per serving (1 piece salmon with 1 generous cup vegetables): 247 Cal, 8 g Fat, 1 g Sat Fat, 77 mg Chol, 638 mg Sod, 12 g Carb, 2 g Fib, 31 g Prot, 52 mg Calc. **POINTS: 5.**

clever cook's tip

Be sure to reserve the juice from the pickled ginger—it's a great flavor booster for dressings, dips, and sauces.

Coconut Rice Pudding

MAKES 6 SERVINGS

This Thai-inspired version of rice pudding is mildly spiced and very creamy. It's excellent served warm and even better the next day chilled with slices of ripe mango.

> 3 cups light coconut milk
> ¾ cup fat-free milk
> ½ cup long-grain white rice
> ¼ cup packed light brown sugar
> 1 teaspoon vanilla extract
> ½ teaspoon ground cinnamon

Combine the coconut milk, milk, rice, and sugar in a medium saucepan. Bring to a simmer, cover, and cook over low heat until the rice is tender and the mixture is creamy, about 1 hour. Remove from the heat; stir in the vanilla and the cinnamon. Serve the pudding warm or chilled.

Per serving (½ cup): 215 Cal, 10 g Fat, 6 g Sat Fat, 1 mg Chol, 40 mg Sod, 26 g Carb, 0 g Fib, 2 g Prot, 53 mg Calc. **POINTS: 5.**

the perfect pantry

These readily available Thai ingredients only sound exotic!
- **Basil:** Fresh herb commonly used in Thai noodle and curry dishes; pungent flavor that's a cross between licorice and cloves.
- **Bean sprouts:** Crisp-tender sprouts of various germinated beans and seeds; mung bean sprouts most commonly used.
- **Coconut milk:** Rich liquid extracted from cooking equal parts water and shredded fresh or desiccated coconut.
- **Hot chili paste:** Thickened mixture made from fermented fava beans, flour, red chiles, and garlic.
- **Jasmine rice:** Variety of aromatic long-grain white rice from Thailand; fragrance similar to that of basmati rice.
- **Lemongrass:** Variety of herb with pale green stalk and long, thin, gray-green leaves; contains same essential oil found in lemon rind; sour-lemon flavor and fragrance; available fresh or dried.
- **Mint:** Fresh herb often used in Thai noodle and curry dishes.
- **Pickled ginger:** Sliced, fresh ginger preserved in sweet vinegar.
- **Rice-paper wrapper:** Edible, translucent sheet of dough made from Asian shrub called rice-paper plant (or rice-paper tree).
- **Rice-stick noodles:** Long, translucent noodles made of rice flour; usually about ¼-inch wide.
- **Thai curry paste:** Blend of chiles, garlic, onion, lemongrass, spices, and shrimp paste.
- **Thai fish sauce (nam pla):** Salty, fermented fish sauce; pungent odor; used as condiment, sauce, and for seasoning.

Coconut Rice Pudding

8

treasures of india

Keema Samosas

MAKES 34 SAMOSAS

A specialty of roadside vendors across India, samosas are savory little pastries filled with vegetables, ground meat or poultry (called keema), or a combination of both. These delicious snacks are traditionally fried, but our ingenious method of replacing the rich dough with wonton wrappers and baking the packages in a hot oven results in the same crispy texture and satisfying taste.

2 tablespoons canola oil

½ cup finely chopped onion

1 jalapeño pepper, seeded and finely chopped (wear gloves to prevent irritation)

2 cloves garlic, minced

1 teaspoon garam masala (Indian spice blend)

¾ teaspoon Madras curry powder

¼ teaspoon ground turmeric

1 pound ground skinless chicken breast

¾ teaspoon salt

3 tablespoons chopped fresh cilantro

1 tablespoon fresh lime juice

34 (3-inch) square wonton wrappers

1. To make the filling, heat a large nonstick skillet over medium-high heat. Swirl in the oil, then add the onion, jalapeño, and garlic. Cook until onion begins to soften, 3–4 minutes. Stir in the garam masala, curry powder, and turmeric; cook 30 seconds. Add the chicken and salt; cook, breaking up the chicken with a wooden spoon, until it is no longer pink, 5–7 minutes. Remove from the heat and stir in the cilantro and lime juice. Cool 10 minutes.

2. Preheat the oven to 425° F. Spray a baking sheet with nonstick spray.

3. Arrange 6 wonton wrappers on a work surface. Place 1 scant tablespoon of the filling in the center of each wrapper. Moisten the edges of each wonton wrapper with water and pull one of the top corners diagonally over the filling to make a triangle. Press the edges firmly to seal. Place completed samosas on the baking sheet in a single layer. Repeat with remaining filling and wrappers, to make 34 samosas.

4. Spray samosas lightly with nonstick spray. Bake, turning once, until crisp and golden, 11–14 minutes.

Per serving (1 samosa): 55 Cal, 1 g Fat, 0 g Sat Fat, 12 mg Chol, 107 mg Sod, 5 g Carb, 0 g Fib, 5 g Prot, 8 mg Calc. **POINTS: 1.**

clever cook's tip

Samosas are a great party food because they freeze in a snap. Prepare the samosas as directed through Step 3. Freeze the samosas on wax or parchment paper–lined baking sheets in single layers, then transfer the frozen samosas to zip-close plastic bags and freeze for up to 2 months. To serve, thaw at room temperature for 15 minutes, then bake as directed.

Mulligatawny Soup

MAKES 6 SERVINGS

Mulligatawny, which means "pepper water," is a highly seasoned specialty soup from southern India. Our spicy version is chock-full of vegetables and enriched with light coconut milk.

- 2 teaspoons canola oil
- 2 carrots, peeled and sliced
- 2 onions, chopped
- 1 celery stalk, chopped
- 3 quarter-size slices peeled fresh ginger
- 3 cloves garlic, minced
- 5 teaspoons Madras curry powder
- ½ teaspoon coriander seeds
- 6 cups low-sodium, fat-free chicken broth
- 1 medium baking potato, peeled and coarsely chopped
- ¾ cup light coconut milk
- 2 tablespoons fresh lime juice
- 3 tablespoons chopped fresh cilantro

1. Heat a large pot over medium-high heat. Swirl in the oil, then add the carrots, onions, celery, ginger, and garlic. Cook until vegetables are softened, 4–5 minutes. Stir in the curry powder and coriander; cook 1 minute. Add the chicken broth and potato. Bring to a boil, cover, and reduce heat to medium-low. Simmer until vegetables are tender, 25 minutes. Remove from the heat and cool 10 minutes.

2. Puree the soup in batches in a blender or food processor. Return soup to the pot, and add the coconut milk and lime juice. Simmer gently over medium-low heat until hot, 8–10 minutes longer. Remove from the heat and stir in the cilantro.

Per serving (1⅓ cups): 117 Cal, 4 Fat, 2 Sat Fat, 0 mg Chol, 672 mg Sod, 17 g Carb, 3 g Fib, 3 g Prot, 36 mg Calc. **POINTS: 2.**

clever cook's tip

This soup can easily be prepared ahead. After pureeing, simply transfer the soup to an airtight container (do not add the cilantro). Let the soup cool at room temperature, then cover and refrigerate it up to 2 days. Heat through just before serving and add the cilantro.

Tandoori Chicken

Tandoori, also known as Indian barbecue, refers to both the yogurt-based marinade and the traditional open-fire tandoor oven made out of brick and clay in which this popular dish is cooked. To replicate the intense heat produced by the tandoor oven in a home kitchen, roast the chicken at a very high temperature.

¾ **cup plain fat-free yogurt**

2 **tablespoons fresh lemon juice**

1 **tablespoon paprika**

2 **teaspoons minced peeled fresh ginger**

1 **clove garlic, minced**

1 **teaspoon ground coriander**

⅛ **teaspoon ground cardamom**

6 **skinless boneless chicken thighs (about 1½ pounds), trimmed of all visible fat**

1. To make the marinade, combine the yogurt, lemon juice, paprika, ginger, garlic, coriander, and cardamom in a large zip-close plastic bag; mix well. Add the chicken, seal the bag, and turn several times to coat. Refrigerate the chicken overnight.

2. Preheat the oven to 500° F. Place a wire rack on a jelly-roll pan. Remove the chicken from the marinade and place on rack; discard marinade. Roast until an instant-read thermometer inserted in the thickest part of the chicken registers 180° F, 35–40 minutes.

Per serving (1 chicken thigh): 184 Cal, 9 g Fat, 3 g Sat Fat, 81 mg Chol, 80 mg Sod, 1 g Carb, 0 g Fib, 23 g Prot, 26 mg Calc. *POINTS: 4.*

clever cook's tip

Oven temperatures can sometimes vary up to 50 degrees, so before getting started it's always a good idea to check your oven's accuracy. Place an oven thermometer on the center rack and preheat the oven for 15 minutes. If the thermometer reading doesn't agree with the oven setting, you'll need to make an adjustment. Use any leftovers to make an Indian-inspired chicken salad. Remove the chicken meat from the bones and cut into cubes. Combine the chicken with some chopped onion and celery, fat-free yogurt, fat-free mayonnaise, ground cumin, curry powder, and fresh lime juice to taste; mix well. Serve with pita bread.

Seek Kebab

This classic Indian dish is thin sausage-shaped kebabs (called seek) made of broiled ground meat and spices. Our version features lean ground turkey with a touch of minced fresh jalapeño and ginger for an extra flavor boost. Serve with our refreshing Cucumber Raita [page 199] or Fresh Mint Chutney [page 200].

1 pound ground skinless turkey breast

1 jalapeño pepper, seeded and finely chopped (wear gloves to prevent irritation)

3 tablespoons chopped fresh cilantro

1 tablespoon minced peeled fresh ginger

2 cloves garlic, minced

1 tablespoon fresh lime juice

1½ teaspoons garam masala

½ teaspoon salt

1. Combine the turkey, jalapeño, cilantro, ginger, garlic, lime juice, garam masala, and salt in a bowl; mix well. Divide mixture into 4 equal portions. Roll each into a 5 x 1½-inch sausage-shaped patty. Refrigerate patties 20 minutes.

2. Meanwhile, preheat oven to 500° F. Coat a baking sheet with nonstick cooking spray; set aside.

3. Insert a metal skewer lengthwise into each patty. Place skewers on the baking sheet. Roast until an instant-read thermometer inserted into each kebab registers 165° F, 12–15 minutes.

Per serving (1 skewer): 145 Cal, 1 g Fat, 0 g Sat Fat, 82 mg Chol, 345 mg Sod, 3 g Carb, 1 g Fib, 30 g Prot, 25 mg Calc. *POINTS: 3.*

clever cook's tip

Get a jump on preparation for a weeknight meal by making Seek Kebab, which can easily be frozen, ahead of time. Prepare the recipe as directed in Step 1, then wrap the patties in double layer of plastic wrap and foil and freeze up to 2 months. Thaw in refrigerator overnight and roast as directed.

treasures of india

Shrimp Vindaloo

MAKES 6 SERVINGS

Vindaloo, a roasted blend of spices and red chiles, is the hottest variety of Indian curries. To avoid the typical mouth-searing affect of take-out vindaloos, we've reduced the heat to a more palatable amount and paired the pungent spice blend with the subtle sweetness of sautéed onions, tomatoes, and shrimp.

1 tablespoon olive oil
2 onions, chopped
1 tablespoon fresh lemon juice
2 teaspoons Madras curry powder
1 teaspoon cumin seeds
⅛ teaspoon cayenne
1½ pounds plum tomatoes, chopped
2 tablespoons sugar
1 tablespoon minced peeled fresh ginger
2 garlic cloves, minced
1½ pounds medium shrimp, peeled and deveined
¾ teaspoon salt

Heat a large nonstick skillet over medium-high heat. Swirl in the oil, then add the onion, lemon juice, curry powder, cumin seeds, and cayenne. Cook, stirring occasionally, until onions soften, 4–5 minutes. Stir in the tomatoes, sugar, ginger, and garlic; cook until tomatoes soften, 5–6 minutes. Add the shrimp and cook until opaque in the center, 4–5 minutes. Stir in the salt and serve at once.

Per serving (1 cup): 155 Cal, 4 g Fat, 1 g Sat Fat, 135 mg Chol, 458 mg Sod, 15 g Carb, 3 g Fib, 16 g Prot, 52 mg Calc. *POINTS: 3.*

clever cook's tip

Fragrant basmati rice and sautéed fresh okra will round out this zesty meal.

Shrimp Vindaloo

Lamb Biriyani

Biriyani, a specialty rice dish from northern India, is prepared with fragrant spices and often includes vegetables and meat. But the key to biriyani's exquisite flavor is basmati rice. Basmati is grown primarily in the foothills of the Himalayan Mountains and is now widely available in the United States in supermarkets and specialty-food stores. It exudes a wonderful aroma while cooking and yields an extra-fluffy, slender grain. Be very gentle when rinsing basmati rice, since rough handling will break the tender grain.

1⅓ cups basmati rice
2 tablespoons canola oil
2 onions, chopped
2 teaspoons cumin seeds
1 teaspoon cinnamon
⅛ teaspoon saffron threads, crushed
⅛ teaspoon cayenne
3 plum tomatoes, chopped
½ cup golden raisins
1 jalapeño pepper, seeded and chopped (wear gloves to prevent irritation)
1 tablespoon minced peeled fresh ginger
2 cloves garlic, minced
1 pound boneless leg of lamb, trimmed of all visible fat, cut into 1-inch cubes
¼ cup chopped mint
2 tablespoons fresh lime juice
1 teaspoon salt
2 cloves

1. To rinse, place the rice in a bowl. Add enough water to cover by several inches and gently swish the grains in the bowl with your fingertips until the water becomes cloudy; drain. Repeat three or four times, until the water is clear.
2. Add enough fresh water to rice to cover by 2 inches. Soak rice 20 minutes; drain.
3. Meanwhile, heat a large saucepan over medium-high heat. Swirl in the oil, then add the onion. Cook, stirring occasionally, until golden, 7–8 minutes. Stir in the cumin, cinnamon, saffron, and cayenne; cook 30 seconds. Add the tomatoes, raisins, jalapeño, ginger, and garlic; cook until tomatoes soften, 3–4 minutes. Add the lamb and cook until lightly browned, 5–7 minutes. Stir in the mint, lime juice, and salt; cook 30 seconds. Add the drained rice and cloves; cook 3 minutes. Add 2 cups water and bring to a boil. Cover, reduce heat to medium-low, and simmer until the liquid is absorbed, 15–18 minutes. Remove the saucepan from the heat and let the rice sit undisturbed for 10 minutes longer.

Per serving (1 cup): 382 Cal, 10 g Fat, 2 g Sat Fat, 48 mg Chol, 437 mg Sod, 54 g Carb, 4 g Fib, 21 g Prot, 48 mg Calc. *POINTS: 8.*

Saag Aloo

MAKES 4 SERVINGS

This classic combination of spiced potatoes and iron-rich greens is a mainstay at most Indian restaurants. But quite often this dish is prepared with ghee, a mixture similar to clarified butter, or quite a bit of oil. Our remedy is to use a scant amount of heart-healthy canola oil and to add sweet red bell peppers and a large handful of chopped fresh mint to replace the fat with sparkling flavor.

1 pound baking potatoes, peeled and cut into ½-inch cubes
2 tablespoons canola oil
1 teaspoon fennel seeds
1 teaspoon cumin seeds
1 medium onion, thinly sliced
1 teaspoon paprika
2 red bell peppers, seeded and thinly sliced
1 tablespoon minced peeled fresh ginger
2 cloves garlic, minced
1 (10-ounce) box frozen chopped spinach, thawed and squeezed dry
2 tablespoons chopped fresh mint
½ teaspoon salt

1. Bring a large pot of lightly salted water to a boil. Add potatoes, return to a boil, and cook until fork-tender, 7 minutes; drain and set aside.

2. Heat a large nonstick skillet over medium-high heat. Swirl in the oil, then add the fennel and cumin seeds. Cook, stirring, until fragrant, 30 seconds. Add the onion and paprika; cook until onion begins to soften, 2–4 minutes. Stir in the bell pepper, ginger, and garlic. Cook, stirring occasionally, until bell pepper begins to soften, 2–3 minutes. Add the potatoes and spinach; cook until spinach is heated though, 2 minutes. Remove from the heat and stir in the mint and salt.

Per serving (¾ cup): 209 Cal, 8 g Fat, 1 g Sat Fat, 0 mg Chol, 629 mg Sod, 33 g Carb, 7 g Fib, 5 g Prot, 141 mg Calc. *POINTS: 4.*

clever cook's tip

Saag Aloo can be made a touch richer and moister with the addition of some light coconut milk. After cooking the spinach for 2 minutes in Step 2, stir in ⅓ to ½ cup light coconut milk and cook until heated through, 30 seconds longer. Stir in the mint and the salt as directed.

treasures of india

Chickpea and Cauliflower Stew

MAKES 4 SERVINGS

Thanks to quick-cooking cauliflower florets, diced potatoes, and canned chickpeas, this hearty stew is ready in less than 30 minutes—making it the perfect weeknight fare. To make this dish a complete protein entrée, serve it with basmati rice.

1½ pounds cauliflower, cut into florets

1 medium baking potato, peeled and cut into ½-inch cubes

2 tablespoons canola oil

2 teaspoons Madras curry powder

1½ teaspoons cumin seeds

⅛ teaspoon cayenne

1 (15½-ounce) can chickpeas (garbanzo beans), rinsed and drained

1 (15-ounce) can crushed tomatoes

1 teaspoon sugar

2 tablespoons chopped fresh cilantro

¼ teaspoon salt

1. Bring a large pot of lightly salted water to a boil. Add the cauliflower and potatoes. Return to a boil and cook 5 minutes; drain and set aside.

2. Meanwhile, heat a large nonstick skillet over medium-high heat. Swirl in the oil, then add the curry powder, cumin, and cayenne. Cook until fragrant, 30 seconds. Add the chickpeas and cook 1 minute. Stir in the crushed tomatoes and sugar; cook 1 minute. Add the cauliflower and potatoes; cook until the tomato sauce thickens and the vegetables are tender, 5–6 minutes longer. Remove from the heat and stir in the cilantro and salt.

Per serving (1 cup plus 3 tablespoons): 238 Cal, 9 g Fat, 1 g Sat Fat, 0 mg Chol, 876 mg Sod, 35 g Carb, 10 g Fib, 9 g Prot, 98 mg Calc.
POINTS: 5.

Dal with Rice and Vegetables

MAKES 4 SERVINGS

Dal, the Hindi word for legumes, covers more than 60 varieties of peas, beans and lentils. Our recipe is prepared with red lentils, subtly flavored with cumin, mustard seeds, and turmeric. The beauty of this dish is that all the ingredients cook in one pot, so clean up is a breeze. Fragrant basmati rice and convenient frozen mixed vegetables round out this vegetarian entrée.

¾ cup basmati or long-grain white rice
3 tablespoons canola oil
1 onion, chopped
1½ teaspoons cumin seeds
¼ teaspoon mustard seeds
1 (10-ounce) box frozen mixed vegetables, thawed
1 tablespoon minced peeled fresh ginger
3 cloves garlic, minced
½ teaspoon ground turmeric
½ cup red lentils, picked over, rinsed, and drained
¾ teaspoon salt
2 tablespoons chopped fresh cilantro

1. To rinse, place the rice in a bowl. Add enough water to cover by several inches and gently swish the grains in the pan with your fingertips until the water becomes cloudy; drain. Repeat three or four times, until the water is clear.

2. Add enough fresh water to rice to cover by 2 inches. Soak rice 20 minutes; drain.

3. Heat a large saucepan over medium-high heat. Swirl in the oil, then add the onion, cumin, and mustard seeds. Cook until onion is softened, 3–4 minutes. Add the mixed vegetables, ginger, garlic, and turmeric; cook 3 minutes. Add the drained rice and lentils; cook 1 minute. Pour in 1⅔ cups water and salt. Bring to a boil, cover, reduce heat to medium-low, and simmer until water is absorbed, 15–18 minutes. Remove the saucepan from the heat, and let the rice sit undisturbed for 10 minutes longer. Stir in the cilantro.

Per serving (1¼ cups): 370 Cal, 11 g Fat, 1 g Sat Fat, 0 mg Chol, 483 mg Sod, 58 g Carb, 8 g Fib, 12 g Prot, 62 mg Calc. ***POINTS: 8.***

clever cook's tip

This dish is a great make-ahead recipe. Prepare as directed (omitting the cilantro), then spread the rice mixture out on a baking sheet and cool to room temperature. Transfer to a plastic container; cover and refrigerate up to 2 days. To reheat, spray a large nonstick skillet with nonstick spray and set over medium heat. Add the rice mixture and cook, stirring often, until heated through, 5–6 minutes. Remove from the heat and stir in the cilantro.

Dal with Spiced
Tomatoes and Potatoes

Dal with Spiced Tomatoes and Potatoes

MAKES 4 SERVINGS

A lovely assortment of lentils, chickpeas, and potatoes is seasoned with garam masala—a spicy and highly aromatic blend of ground cardamom, cinnamon, cloves, and black pepper. Like many other dals, this dish is rather starchy, so feel free to add a little tomato juice or water if you prefer a moister texture.

- 1 medium baking potato, peeled and cut into ½-inch cubes
- ¼ cup red lentils, picked over, rinsed, and drained
- 2 tablespoons canola oil
- 1 onion, chopped
- 1 jalapeño pepper, seeded and chopped (wear gloves to prevent irritation)
- 1¼ teaspoons garam masala
- 1 teaspoon cumin seeds
- 1 pound plum tomatoes, chopped
- 1 (15½-ounce) can chickpeas (garbanzo beans), rinsed and drained
- 1 tablespoon peeled minced fresh ginger
- 2 cloves garlic, minced
- 1 tablespoon chopped fresh cilantro

1. Bring a large saucepan of lightly salted water to a boil. Add potatoes, return to a boil, and cook until fork-tender, 7 minutes; remove with a slotted spoon and set aside, reserving the cooking liquid.

2. Add lentils to the same saucepan and return cooking liquid to a boil. Cook until lentils are tender but still hold their shape, 8–10 minutes; drain and set aside.

3. Heat a large nonstick skillet over medium-high heat. Swirl in the oil, then add the onion, jalapeño, garam masala, and cumin. Cook until onion begins to soften, 3–4 minutes. Stir in the potatoes, tomatoes, chickpeas, ginger, and garlic. Cook, stirring occasionally, until tomatoes soften and potatoes are tender, 4–5 minutes. Stir in lentils and cook until heated through, 1 minute. Remove from the heat and stir in cilantro.

Per serving (1 cup): 247 Cal, 9 g Fat, 1 g Sat Fat, 0 mg Chol, 335 mg Sod, 36 g Carb, 8 g Fib, 9 g Prot, 64 mg Calc. *POINTS: 5.*

clever cook's tip

Garam masala may be purchased in Indian markets and in the spice aisle of some supermarkets.

Pullao

Pullao, or pilaf, is basmati rice cooked with spices, meat, chicken, or vegetables. Our version highlights the flavor intensity of whole spices—cardamom, cloves, cinnamon, and bay leaf—with the simple addition of bright green peas and caramelized onions.

1 cup basmati or long-grain white rice

½ cup frozen peas, thawed

2 cardamom pods

2 cloves

1 cinnamon stick

1 bay leaf

¾ teaspoon salt

½ teaspoon cumin seeds

1 tablespoon canola oil

1 onion, thinly sliced

1. To rinse, place the rice in a medium saucepan. Add enough water to cover by several inches and gently swish the grains in the pan with your fingertips until the water becomes cloudy; drain. Repeat three or four times, until the water is clear.

2. Combine rice with 1¾ cups fresh water; let stand 20 minutes.

3. Bring the rice mixture to a boil over medium-high heat. Stir in the peas, cardamom, cloves, cinnamon stick, bay leaf, salt, and cumin. Cover, reduce heat to low, and simmer until liquid is absorbed, 15–18 minutes. Remove the saucepan from the heat, and let the rice sit undisturbed 10 minutes longer.

4. Meanwhile, heat a large nonstick skillet over high heat. Swirl in the oil, then add the onion. Cook, stirring often, until the onion is golden brown, 6–8 minutes. Garnish rice with onions.

Per serving (1 cup): 157 Cal, 3 g Fat, 0 g Sat Fat, 0 mg Chol, 306 mg Sod, 30 g Carb, 2 g Fib, 4 g Prot, 11 mg Calc. ***POINTS: 3.***

clever cook's tip

Cardamom pods come in three varieties—green, white, and black. Green and white are the most widely available at supermarkets and gourmet stores. Although we prefer the more intense aroma of natural green cardamom (the white variety has been bleached), either can be used in this recipe.

Chapati

MAKES 12 BREADS

Most of the breads eaten in Indian homes are a simple mixture of unleavened whole-grain flour, water, and salt. Baked breads like chapati, which are prepared on a griddle or over an open fire, are among the most popular. Warm and crisp, chapati makes a wonderful accompaniment to any Indian meal.

1⅓ cups whole-wheat flour
⅔ cup all-purpose flour
½ teaspoon salt
¾ cup warm water

1. Combine the whole-wheat flour, all-purpose flour, and salt in a large bowl. Make a well in the center of the flour mixture and slowly pour in the water, mixing with your fingers to form a dough.

2. Turn the dough out onto a well-floured surface and knead until smooth, soft, and pliable, 7–10 minutes. Cover dough and let it rest 10 minutes.

3. Divide dough into 12 equal portions. Under the palm of your hand, roll each piece of dough into a ball. Working one ball at a time, roll each into a 6- to 7-inch circle.

4. Heat a heavy-bottomed skillet over medium-high heat until hot but not smoking. Place one dough circle in the skillet, and press it down with a spatula. Cook until the top is bubbled and the bottom is lightly browned. Turn the chapati over; press with the spatula and cook 1 minute longer. Remove from the skillet and keep warm. Repeat with remaining dough to make 12 chapati.

Per serving (1 chapati): 71 Cal, 0 g Fat, 0 g Sat Fat, 0 mg Chol, 98 mg Sod, 15 g Carb, 2 g Fib, 3 g Prot, 6 mg Calc. *POINTS: 1.*

clever cook's tip

Chapati can be made up to 1 day ahead—a great help for weeknight cooking. Simply cool the breads completely, wrap in foil, then refrigerate. To reheat, prepare chapati as directed in Step 4, except cook each bread, one at a time, until heated through, 30–60 seconds on each side.

treasures of india

Chapati, Cucumber Raita, Mango Lassi, and Fresh Mint Chutney

Cucumber Raita

MAKES 12 SERVINGS

An Indian meal, especially if it's vegetarian, isn't complete unless it includes yogurt—a primary source of protein. Raita, or yogurt salad, is an easy and convenient way to get these essential nutrients. Traditionally raita is made with ultrarich buffalo's-milk yogurt, but we've substituted low-fat yogurt. This refreshing recipe, with cucumber and fresh mint, is the perfect condiment to serve with any spicy dish.

---

2 cups plain
low-fat yogurt

2 cucumbers, peeled,
seeded, grated,
and squeezed dry

½ jalapeño pepper,
seeded and thinly
sliced (wear gloves
to prevent irritation)

2 tablespoons
chopped fresh mint

1 teaspoon ground
cumin

¾ teaspoon salt

¼ teaspoon ground
coriander

---

1. Spoon the yogurt into a coffee filter or a cheesecloth-lined strainer; set over a bowl and let stand and strain for 20 minutes. Discard the liquid.

2. Combine the strained yogurt, cucumbers, jalapeño, mint, cumin, salt, and coriander in a bowl; mix well.

Per serving (¼ cup): 32 Cal, 1 g Fat, 0 g Sat Fat, 3 mg Chol, 175 mg Sod, 4 g Carb, 0 g Fib, 2 g Prot, 83 mg Calc. *POINTS: 1.*

clever cook's tip

Raita's flavors will actually improve if refrigerated in an airtight container overnight and served the next day. It will remain fresh and flavorful refrigerated up to 1 week.

Fresh Mint Chutney

MAKES 4 SERVINGS ◊ ⏱

This is the most popular chutney in north India, where fresh mint flourishes year-round. The relish has the thick, pesto-like consistency and is wonderful served with lamb, chicken, seafood, or as a dipping sauce with our Keema Samosas [page 184]. It's also great stirred into some plain fat-free yogurt and served with Chapati [page 197] or other flat breads.

2 cups loosely packed fresh mint leaves (about 2 bunches)
½ jalapeño pepper, seeded and chopped (wear gloves to prevent irritation)
2 tablespoons chopped fresh cilantro
2 tablespoons chopped onion
1 tablespoon fresh lime juice
2 teaspoons grated lime rind
2 teaspoons sugar
1 teaspoon peeled minced fresh ginger
½ teaspoon salt

Combine the mint leaves, jalapeño, cilantro, onion, lime juice, lime rind, sugar, ginger, and salt in a blender or food processor. Blend until smooth.

Per serving (2 tablespoons): 34 Cal, 0 g Fat, 0 g Sat Fat, 0 mg Chol, 306 mg Sod, 7 g Carb, 3 g Fib, 2 g Prot, 95 mg Calc. *POINTS: 0.*

clever cook's tip

This recipe easily doubles, and any extra can be refrigerated up to 3 days. Transfer the chutney to an airtight container and press a piece of plastic wrap directly onto the surface. Keep in mind that the longer the chutney sits the more assertive it will taste as the flavors meld.

Mango Lassi

Ice-cold lassi is a sweetened yogurt drink that is served throughout India. Frothy, creamy, and scented with fresh mango, it can be enjoyed any time of day.

2 ripe mangoes, peeled, pitted, and cubed	Combine the mangoes, yogurt, milk, sugar, and ice cubes in a blender. Pulse on high speed until the mixture is thick and smooth. Pour the lassi into 4 glasses and garnish with mint sprigs (if using).
1½ cups plain low-fat yogurt	
1 cup fat-free milk	
6 tablespoons sugar	
6 ice cubes	
Fresh mint sprigs (optional)	

2 ripe mangoes, peeled, pitted, and cubed
1½ cups plain low-fat yogurt
1 cup fat-free milk
6 tablespoons sugar
6 ice cubes
Fresh mint sprigs (optional)

Combine the mangoes, yogurt, milk, sugar, and ice cubes in a blender. Pulse on high speed until the mixture is thick and smooth. Pour the lassi into 4 glasses and garnish with mint sprigs (if using).

Per serving (1¼ cups): 171 Cal, 2 g Fat, 1 g Sat Fat, 7 mg Chol, 98 mg Sod, 33 g Carb, 2 g Fib, 7 g Prot, 254 mg Calc. *POINTS: 3.*

clever cook's tip

For a last-minute treat, blend the ingredients as directed, except omit the ice cubes. Refrigerate up to 2 hours. When ready to serve, add the ice and blend again until thick and smooth.

the perfect pantry

Here are the spices, grains, and more you'll need to create traditional Indian fare.
•**Basmati rice:** Delicate, long-grain white rice from the Himalayas with a nutlike flavor and aroma.
•**Cardamom:** Aromatic spice native to India; used ground or in whole pods; pungent aroma, warm spicy-sweet flavor.
•**Chickpeas (garbanzo beans):** Round ivory legume often used in Indian dishes; firm texture; mild nutlike flavor.
•**Coconut milk:** Rich liquid extracted from cooking equal parts water and shredded fresh or desiccated coconut.
•**Coriander:** Fragrant, aromatic spice; flavor suggests a combination of lemon, sage, and caraway.
•**Cumin:** Aromatic, nutty-flavored spice used alone or to make curry powder.
•**Garam masala:** Blend of dry-roasted, ground spices that can include black pepper, cinnamon, cloves, coriander, cumin, cardamom, chiles, fennel, mace, or nutmeg.
•**Madras curry powder:** Curry powder is a blend of up to 20 ground spices, herbs, and seeds; Madras is a hotter variety of curry powder.
•**Mustard seeds:** Seeds from mustard greens, of which there are two major varieties: white (or yellow) and brown (or Asian); brown seeds more pungent.
•**Red lentils:** Small, round, reddish-orange variety of lentil often used in Indian dishes.
•**Turmeric:** Bitter, pungent-flavored spice with an intense yellow-orange color; used to flavor and color dishes and to make curry powder.

treasures of india

index

DRY AND LIQUID MEASUREMENT EQUIVALENTS

If you are converting the recipes in this magazine to metric measurements, use the following chart as a guide.

TEASPOONS	TABLESPOONS	CUPS	FLUID OUNCES
3 teaspoons	1 tablespoon		½ fluid ounce
6 teaspoons	2 tablespoons	⅛ cup	1 fluid ounce
8 teaspoons	2 tablespoons plus 2 teaspoons	⅙ cup	
12 teaspoons	4 tablespoons	¼ cup	2 fluid ounces
15 teaspoons	5 tablespoons	⅓ cup minus 1 teaspoon	2 fluid ounces
16 teaspoons	5 tablespoons plus 1 teaspoon	⅓ cup	
18 teaspoons	6 tablespoons	¼ cup plus 2 tablespoons	3 fluid ounces
24 teaspoons	8 tablespoons	½ cup	4 fluid ounces
30 teaspoons	10 tablespoons	½ cup plus 2 tablespoons	5 fluid ounces
32 teaspoons	10 tablespoons plus 2 teaspoons	⅔ cup	
36 teaspoons	12 tablespoons	¾ cup	6 fluid ounces
42 teaspoons	14 tablespoons	1 cup minus 1 tablespoon	7 fluid ounces
45 teaspoons	15 tablespoons	1 cup minus 1 tablespoon	
48 teaspoons	16 tablespoons	1 cup	8 fluid ounces

Note: Measurement of less than ⅛ teaspoon is considered a dash or a pinch.

VOLUME	
¼ teaspoon	1 milliliter
½ teaspoon	2 milliliters
1 teaspoon	5 milliliters
1 tablespoon	15 milliliters
2 tablespoons	20 milliliters
3 tablespoons	45 milliliters
¼ cup	60 milliliters
⅓ cup	75 milliliters
½ cup	125 milliliters
⅔ cup	150 milliliters
¾ cup	175 milliliters
⅔ cup	150 milliliters
1 cup	225 milliliters
1 quart	150 liters

OVEN TEMPERATURE	
250°F	120°C
275°F	140°C
300°F	150°C
325°F	160°C
350°F	180°C
375°F	190°C
400°F	200°C
425°F	220°C
450°F	230°C
475°F	250°C
500°F	260°C
525°F	270°C

WEIGHT	
1 ounce	30 grams
¼ pound	120 grams
½ pound	240 grams
¾ pound	360 grams

LENGTH	
1 inch	25 millimeters
1 inch	2.5 centimeters

notes

notes

notes